an introduction
to human –
communication
theory

Speech Communication Series

an introduction to human- communication theory

George A. Borden
The Pennsylvania State University

WM. C. BROWN COMPANY PUBLISHERS, *Dubuque, Iowa*

SPEECH SERIES

Consulting Editor
Baxter M. Geeting
Sacramento State College

Copyright © 1971 by
Wm. C. Brown Company Publishers

ISBN 0–697–04109–3

Library of Congress Catalog Card Number: 75-136239

Printed in the United States of America

Dynamic developments of our time, particularly the communication explosion and new revelations concerning human behavior, demand fresh approaches to the teaching of speech. Modern life places an emphasis on speech as an *act of communication,* interdisciplinary in nature, capable of adding new dimensions to man's evolution and progress in all areas of life. The SPEECH COMMUNICATION SERIES, addressed to the introductory student, represents a significant attempt to provide new materials for today's teaching needs.

Basic to all titles in the series is the desire to present the material in the clearest and most lucid style for the purpose of making speech communication a useful, ethical and satisfying experience. While the individual titles are self-contained, collectively they provide the substance for a comprehensive study of those topics fundamental to a basic course in speech communication.

GRATEFULLY
DEDICATED
TO
darlene
esther
mary
charlotte
bea

PREFACE

There is great need for each of us to understand the human-communication process. Present unrest throughout the world in general and on the college campuses in particular is ample evidence of human-communication problems. To understand and alleviate these problems, one must know more about the why's and how's of man's communicative behavior. This book is written as an introduction to the theories applicable to the study of human communication. It is not an introductory theory of human communication, though its organization may suggest such a theory.

It is hoped that this book will help the reader to think more deeply about the many facets of the communication process. It was written to be used as the source for discussion in a class involved in the study of any phase of human communication. It does not try to answer questions —hopefully, it will raise them. Then, together, the student and teacher may search for the best possible answers. To aid in this endeavor, the text is sprinkled liberally with discussion topics which attempt to guide both student and teacher into the richer areas of research and discussion.

The plan of the text is to use the individual as the central unit in the communication process. Thus, we try to conceptualize this process in terms of the individual's role in it (Chapter 1); we then look at the historical attempts to study this process (Chapter 2); the psychoneurological basis for communication (Chapter 3); the theories of cognition developed to explain human behavior (Chapter 4); the theories explaining human communicative behavior (Chapter 5); and the use of the concept of literacy to focus in on the human-communication process (Chapter 6). At the end of each of these chapters, there is a selected bibliography of books that should be available in any college or university library. These should be consulted for further explication of the theories to which we have referred.

CONTENTS

Chapter 1

A CONCEPTUALIZATION OF THE HUMAN-COMMUNICATION PROCESS

"They got me to the hospital, slit my throat and stuck a pump down to take this stuff out of my lungs—which if you molded it into a ball and threw it on the floor it would bounce. I did come to on the operating table. Everybody had green caps, green masks, green outfits and this huge, blazing light was over my head. I tried to say the usual bromide, 'Where am I?' But the breath just blew out the gash in my throat—a big wound mouth. I couldn't even whisper. Now you can't imagine how terrifying that is. That's when I thought maybe I was dead. Then I became aware of this terrible contraption and that I couldn't move. My whole body was paralyzed. But I guess my eyelids were moving, my mouth was trying to move. I don't know how long nobody noticed—I screamed inside—like one of those awful science-fiction stories you read, of somebody waking up in a coffin.

"Finally one of the nurses saw that my eyes were open and there must have been a look of such terror in my eyes, because she bent over and told me that I was at the London Clinic and that I was going to be all right. And I knew I was going to die. I gestured that I wanted to write something, because the feeling of being unable to communicate was more frightening than anything. And I wrote, 'Am I still dying?' And the writing looked like a 190-year-old creature—it took up a whole page. Then I went into another coma."[1]

Do you believe the statement, ". . . the feeling of being unable to communicate was more frightening than anything."? If you have ever had a similar experience, you probably already realize that being unable to communicate, and realizing it, is undoubtedly the worst condi-

---

1. From "Elizabeth Taylor Speaks Out," by Richard Meryman, *Life* Magazine, December 18, 1964 © 1964, *Time, Inc.*

tion a human being can be in. We need only reflect on the stories of Edgar Allen Poe or on other horror stories to realize that this is one of man's greatest fears. In fact, it probably is the basis of nearly all of man's fears.

Now we should ask ourselves why: What is it about human communication that makes it so essential to man? If you are psychologically introverted, you may say, "Who needs to communicate? I would get along just fine if I never spoke to anyone." On the other hand, if you are more extroverted, you may feel that you have to have someone to talk to all the time or you will go crazy. Probably, most of you fall somewhere in between and thus have times when you want to be left alone and times when you want to talk to someone. In any case, whether you are introverted, extroverted, or "normal," if your ability to communicate is suddenly lost, you will feel that you no longer have any contact with reality and will probably react in some way similar to the way that Miss Taylor reacted.

One important ingredient in human communication, then, is a feeling of contact with reality. We usually get this feeling by communicating with fellow human beings, though Thoreau has shown us that this is not the only way.[2] Yet, as a general statement, we may say that communication involves people. Colin Cherry says, "Communication renders true social life practicable, for communication means organization."[3] Through communication, man is able to influence man and, hopefully, bring order out of chaos (though at times we are made to wonder). Cherry goes on to say, "Communication means a sharing of elements of behavior, or modes of life, by the existence of sets of rules."[4] Social rules and human behavior sometimes communicate more readily than does the language we use. When human beings interact either verbally or nonverbally, they are informing each other of their ways of life, telling each other what and how they think and by what rules they are governed.

Man is basically a social animal; he desires companionship. He is unable to live in complete isolation. If he must be alone, his mind soon begins to play tricks on him, and if he is not taken out of his isolation, he will go mad. Reflect on the fact that solitary confinement is considered extreme punishment. The fear of being alone often causes man to do strange things. Our sense receptors seem to become hypersensitive, for we become aware of all sorts of noises. Our thought processes race madly from one idea to another as though they were trying to find some new information to process. However, the addition of one other live ingredient into this situation usually calms the nerves and abates the

---

2. Henry David Thoreau, *Walden* (New York: The New American Library, 1960).
3. Colin Cherry, *On Human Communication* (Cambridge: The M.I.T. Press, 1957), p. 4.
4. Ibid., p. 6.

fears. Single people, not wanting to live completely alone, adopt pets of one kind or another and soon begin talking to them and treating them much as they would a human being. Many people marry only because they do not want to be alone. Could it be that the need to communicate is a drive that is nearly as basic as respiration or hunger, and more basic than sex?

Discuss the hierarchy of human needs.

Having established that communication, whatever it is, is an important activity in the human being's daily life, let us now proceed to the task of defining what we mean by the word communication. One could refer to many books that have been written about communication and extract from these books the authors' definitions of communication, but it is doubtful that such a procedure would impress upon the reader's mind the real magnitude of the area of knowledge contained in the single concept, communication. Therefore, we will attempt to examine the several bits and pieces of communication to see if we can pull from these truncated processes a few ideas of what communication is all about.

It should be noted that Miss Taylor's first conscious attempt to communicate was by means of spoken discourse. We say conscious, because it is obvious that she had been communicating to her doctors unconsciously for some time and that she had continued to communicate to them when she slipped back into a coma after the episode recorded earlier. Much of this unconscious communication played a vital role in her own well-being, for it enabled the physicians to treat her condition wisely and immediately. Without the unconscious communication, it is doubtful that she would have survived this ordeal. These considerations make us raise the question of intent in communication. Must one consciously intend to communicate with another for it to be said that communication has occurred? The answer is an emphatic No! Think of the numerous ways in which we communicate with those with whom we come in contact each day. Our appearance, activities, facial expressions, and the like are constantly being monitored by those around us.

Discuss several ways in which one may communicate unconsciously.

A book published by Pan American World Airways, *Passports and Profits,* written by Richard G. Lurie, illustrates that nonverbal communication is as important as verbal communication. He says,

After work, an American executive on business in Germany may be invited to an associate's home for dinner. Take flowers, they are advised, but make sure they aren't red roses; they would indicate "you are secretly in love with the hostess."

Maybe the American business traveler will be invited to dinner by a Moroccan businessman. Says the book: "It's the custom to eat with your fingers, but don't grab the food—just use the first three fingers of your right, never your left, hand. After dinner—and after your third glass of mint tea—it's time to leave."

In Japan, "entertaining does not necessarily mean business acceptance. They want to know you, to see how you react to a social situation. . . . Be on your best behavior on these entertainment sorties—no familiarity, back-slapping, first names, or pinching the Geisha girls."[5]

Differences in culture may result in many embarrassing situations that are completely unintended by either party to the communication.[6] It may be noticed that much of the unintended communication occurs, not via spoken discourse, but by what we see.

It is safe to say that one can never be completely sure as to what he has communicated to another person. From the receiver's point of view, he can never be positive that he has interpreted the correct meaning from any signal he has received. If we accept this uncertainty, we may define communication to mean that a person is affected by some external stimulus. Thus, a listener can be sure (usually) when communication has occurred, but he cannot be sure that it has occurred exactly as the communicator wished. This may be because the communicator is transmitting many more signals than the one he intends to communicate, for example, bringing roses says that I appreciate your hospitality, but the color of the roses says something else; or it may be because the receiver misinterprets the intended message, for example, a slap on the back should be interpreted as a friendly gesture but is not always so interpreted.

Although most textbooks as well as other books—some of them widely read, dealing with the subject of communication have approached the subject entirely from the viewpoint of language, or have emphasized this aspect of the communication process to the point that one tends to think only in terms of language when he thinks of communication, it is necessary to realize that there are many ways of expressing oneself other than by language. We will take a much broader approach to communication than the traditional one and launch our study from the pad constructed by Warren Weaver when he defined communication to "include all of the procedures by which one mind may affect another. This, of course, involves not only written and oral speech, but also music, the pictorial arts, the theatre, the ballet, and, in fact, all human behavior."[7] This makes it necessary to insist that communication takes place whenever a person reacts to a stimulus, whether

---

5. Excerpt taken from "The Tactful Traveler," in *The National Observer* (December 21, 1964).

6. Edward T. Hall, *The Silent Language* (Premier Book, d117) is a very readable exposition of unintended communication. That time, space, and culture communicate are only a few of the points made in this book.

7. Claude Shannon and Warren Weaver, *The Mathematical Theory of Communication* (Urbana, Ill.: University of Illinois Press, 1962), p. 95.

he is conscious of this reaction or not. It rules out the necessity of either conscious perception of a stimulus or conscious intent to respond and thus to communicate with another. The example of Miss Taylor illustrates the necessity for making the definition of communication so all-inclusive. While she was on the operating table, even though she was in a coma, she was communicating to the doctors at her side. Had she not been actively communicating through her natural body activity, she would have been pronounced dead. Perhaps the fact to be pointed out here is that communication may occur on many different levels.

Discuss the implications of this multilevel approach to human communication.

The implications of such an all-inclusive definition tend to stagger our imaginations, but the definition also allows us to see the importance of studying this phenomenon called communication. It should also make us aware of the impossibility of knowing all there is to know about human communication but, at the same time, it should make us realize the importance of being aware of the many ways in which communication may occur. The subtleness of the communication process can be shown in many different ways. One may be shown how a person reacts to stimuli that he does not realize he is receiving,[8] or how he misinterprets the stimuli that he consciously receives.[9]

A schema of the communication process may help to solidify this point.

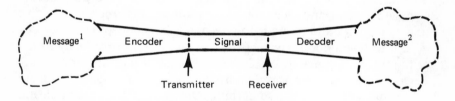

FIGURE 1

A Communication Schema

A communicator has a message he would like to communicate to a communicatee. To communicate this message (Message [1]), he must first put it into a code (the process of Encoding) which can be transmitted to the communicatee. We call this transmitted coded message a

---

8. Vance Packard has given abundant evidence of this in his book, *The Hidden Persuaders* (Picket Books 75027), and every packager of produce and every store manager or salesman must be constantly aware of this phenomenon.

9. The mentally ill are, of course, prime examples of the latter communication difficulty. And yet one does not have to rely on the fringes of sanity to illustrate this point. The well over 300 divisions of so-called Christianity, all supposedly taking their authority from the Bible, are ample evidence that misinterpretation is a common occurrence among human beings.

Signal. When the signal is received by the communicatee, he must decipher this code (the process of Decoding) and allow it to evoke meaning in his own mind (Message [2]). The degree to which Message [1] is congruent with Message [2] is a measure of the communicative effectiveness of the communicator. One should see immediately that any message may be put into several different codes, and, in fact, the signal transmitted in almost every communicative situation is a composite of several codes all of which should complement the primary code of the signal. Thus, our verbal and nonverbal actions should both be "saying" the same thing. When they are not, then there is unnecessary noise in the system, and our communicative effectiveness is diminished.

Discuss explicit examples of complementary and competing codes in given communication situations.

If one looks carefully at each example of communication given so far, he will see that, in each case, there is an originator (communicator) and a recipient (communicatee) in the communication process. It is acknowledged that these two entities may, in fact, be combined in one individual, but it should be noticed that Miss Taylor found that she was unable to realize the existence of this condition. Without some overt interaction with the outside world, one soon finds himself wondering if he is even thinking. For our purposes, then, we may say that, in the communication process, there is always an originator, a recipient and, of course, the thing that is transmitted and received—the signal. The division of the communication process into these three entities— originator, signal, and recipient—oversimplifies this process, but it gives us a convenient and immediately recognizable concept of the process.

Let us begin our analysis of the communication process by looking at the entity designated "originator." Notice, if you will, that in Miss Taylor's episode, there was a desire on her part to say something and, when this failed, to write something. One part of the communication process, then, must be behavioral, that is, it is an expressive action on the part of the one who initiates the communiqué. In this case, the expressive action was desired by the communicator but, as we saw in the excerpts from *Passports and Profits,* the expressive actions could very well be unintentional. In either case, there is a definite phase of the communication process that one can descriptively call the expressive action phase, that is, a phase in which signals are transmitted.

The next step in the analysis is to look at the entity designated "recipient" and, as one would expect, there are, in this phase of the communication process, equal but opposite actions to those of the expressive phase. Man's senses are continually receiving signals from the outside world and passing them on to his brain. All, or most, of these signals may be unintended by the communicator; they may not even be desired by the receiver, but they are received nevertheless. In the cases of the foreign gentlemen who placed their American friends in certain positions to see how they would react, there was a conscious desire on their part to receive information about the Americans. However, almost everyone has overheard a conversation or seen a gift unintentionally and, thus, has received information that was undesired and irrevocable. This information receiving or gathering phase may be designated the "reception" phase of the communication process, and it should be abundantly clear that this part of the process may also be intentional or unintentional.

The third entity identified in the communication process, designated "signal," should be clarified at this time. When Miss Taylor tried to talk, the only perceivable indications were the sound of air coming from the slit in her throat and the movement of her lips and eyes. When she attempted to transmit this signal by writing, she found that she had very little control over her ability to communicate what she desired. The American businessman may find himself in an embarrassing predicament because he has initiated a signal that he did not intend, or because he has interpreted another's signal incorrectly. The result of unintelligible, unintended, or misinterpreted signals may be a serious problem for either the communicator, the communicatee, or both.

One might legitimately ask why so much ambiguity may surround the signal phase of the communication process. If we recall that the signal is composed of many complementing and/or distracting codes, we are immediately aware of part of the problem. Distracting codes make it more difficult to focus on the primary code and, thus, confuse the recipient of the signal. At the same time, it must be realized that a code (language) is made up of elements (words) which are symbols (representations) of the real world. No two people have the same referent for any given symbol. The fact that all signals are symbolic means that each individual will decode a slightly different message from any given signal. Thus, communication is, at best, approximate.

Discuss ways in which signals may be disambiguated.

Much of the analysis of the signal phase of the communication process is studied under the discipline called rhetoric. Since this discipline is well over 2,500 years old, it is not strange that rhetoricians have gained some insights into this phase of the communication process. The fundamentals of the rhetorical process will be covered in the next chapter, but in this chapter, we shall limit our remarks to an intuitive analysis of the signal phase. This analysis begins with the realization that the signal as an entity may exist in isolation. However, so far as communication is concerned, it is meaningless to talk about a signal separate and apart from an originator and a recipient. The truth of this statement is more evident if the reader allows himself the liberty of stepping from one culture into another. The simple waving of the hand to the Japanese means "Come here," but to Americans, it means "hi," or "goodby." Thus, the signal cannot be considered without discussing its interpretations. On closer analysis, one sees that the signal may not only be misinterpreted, but that it may not even be received correctly.

To discuss the signal phase of the communication process, one must also investigate the mechanisms by which one interprets this signal. The interpretation of any signal is contingent upon the experiences one has had with similar signals. One has only to reflect for a moment to discover the role experience plays in the interpretation of a signal. The propagation of the many different denominations of the Protestant religion with their many subdivisions indicates quite clearly that the early experience of the communicant has much to do with the way he interprets the Bible. The experience of the recipient is a major factor in the meaning evoked by any given signal. Thus, the interpretation of a signal is a very subjective thing.

We have now distinguished three entities in the communication process—the originator, the signal, and the recipient. Communication takes place when an originator transmits a signal which the recipient receives and interprets. This is a very simple model of the communication process and also a very limited definition of communication. One may design many different models to illustrate the mechanics of human communication. We shall look at a few to see if we can better understand what goes on during the human-communication process.

COMMUNICATION MODELS

In the previous section, we attempted to define communication by indicating when it *did* or *did not* occur. From these examples, certain facts about communication were obtainable. However, it is difficult to study the concept of communication if one looks only at examples of communication and does not attempt to describe what it is he is looking at. When one attempts to analyze or explain what it is he is considering, he must of necessity form some theory about what he thinks is going on and thus delineate the important facets or phases of the process. This procedure usually leads to a deeper understanding of the concept under consideration and, thus, enlightens all concerned.

Perhaps one may best indicate what communication is by presenting a schema of the process in general. The classic attempt at schematizing the communication process was by Warren Weaver in his analysis of the importance of Claude Shannon's treatise on the mathematics of information theory.[10] His first symbolic representation was as follows:

---

10. Claude Shannon and Warren Weaver, *The Mathematical Theory of Communication* (Urbana, Ill.: University of Illinois Press, 1962), p. 98.

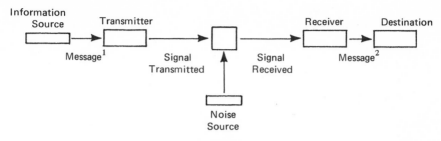

FIGURE 2
The Shannon-Weaver Schema

The Information Source encodes the desired message. For example, the brain of Miss Taylor chose the words "Where am I?" and the Transmitter ordinarily would have sent this signal out over the air in the form of sound waves. But in the case of Miss Taylor, her vocal mechanism, that is, the Transmitter, was unable to send out this signal because of its inability to function properly. When Miss Taylor's normal method of communicating was interrupted, her brain encoded a different message, "Am I still dying," and she attempted to transmit this in a slightly different manner, that is, by writing the signal on a piece of paper. In each case, the specific transmitter being employed by Miss Taylor attempted to transmit the signal she wanted to send via the proper media for that transmitter. The fact remains that she could not transmit the signal via one media and had difficulty sending it via the other. Had she been able to speak, it is questionable whether or not her signal would have reached any of the receivers unaltered, for the actual existence of noise in the room may have interfered with the reception of the exact signal. The receiver, that is, the ears or eyes of the listener, must then take the signal (coded message) and send it to the brain where it is decoded into something the destination can understand.

In order to get understanding or meaning from a signal (and also to put a definite meaning into a signal), Weaver hypothesized another model with a "semantic receiver" between the receiver and the destination, and "semantic noise" between the source and the transmitter. However, we may revise Weaver's schema somewhat to incorporate psychological terminology. We may substitute for information source the word "stimulus," for semantic noise the term "semantic encoder," for semantic receiver the term "semantic decoder," and for destination the word "response." These changes, plus a few other modifications, give a schema as shown on page 10.

Perhaps an analysis of this model will indicate to the reader some of the things that go on during the communication process. When looking at the communication process in this way, one must have a

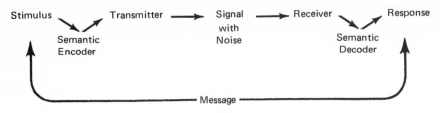

FIGURE 3

A Psychological Schema

starting point. The logical starting point is the "cause" of the communicative act. This cause is invariably another communicative act, thus implying that the process of communication is continuous and, in reality, cannot be broken into discrete acts. However, for the purposes of analysis, we will lift a piece of communication out of the continuing process and look at it as a discrete act. We have designated the beginning of this truncated process as stimulus. This may be anything from a pin prick (to which we transmit the word "ouch" or some other suitable epithet, depending upon the force of the stimulus and the "nature" of our semantic encoding process) to a desire to express the beauty of the Colorado Rockies (to which we transmit, according to our varying abilities, a landscape painting, a poem, or a detailed description). The stimulus which starts us on the way to communicating may be anything received, either consciously or unconsciously.

If our senses receive something and we decide to respond overtly, the shape of this response will be controlled by the nature of our semantic encoder. One may say, quite categorically, that everything we do is filtered through a semantic filter where the meaning of the stimulus we have received is placed into some sort of human behavior which we will transmit and which, in turn, will evoke some meaning in the person or persons with whom we are communicating. In this particular step, we are taking meaning and putting it into some kind of signal which we will transmit to someone else. The transmission of this signal then becomes our response to the initial stimulus. We may schematize this as follows:

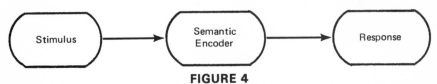

FIGURE 4

An Individual's Schema

The semantic encoder, then, may be viewed as being much like a synthesizer which takes the raw material and shapes it into something that will be recognizable by those with whom it comes in contact. We call this thing a signal, and it should be obvious to the reader that the signal one person produces from a given stimulus may be somewhat different from the signal another person produces from the same stimulus. This phenomenon, we will say, is due to the differences in the experiences of these two people. These experiences are in some way responsible for the particular form of the signals transmitted by the person doing the communicating. The semantic encoder, then, may be a hypothetical device which transforms any given stimulus into an appropriate signal to be transmitted by the individual initiating the communiqué.

Discuss several examples of what would happen if this semantic encoder were to malfunction.

As soon as the signal is formed, or perhaps as soon as it is deemed necessary to transmit something, the transmitter will begin to emit this signal. In the case of spoken discourse, the transmitter is the vocal mechanism plus the bodily action that takes place during the transmission. For written discourse, the transmitter would be the appendage that manipulates the writing instrument. One should be able to give examples of malfunctions in this phase of the communication process, also. In the example that has been used, Miss Taylor's vocal transmitter would not function at all, and her writing ability was impaired by her physical and mental condition. We have all been subjected to the admonition, "Don't talk with your mouth full." What happens when one disobeys this basic principle? Usually, his intended signal is misunderstood, and the meaning that is evoked in the mind of the listener is that this person has poor manners. The transmitter, then, may also inject misunderstanding into the process of communication.

After the signal leaves the communicator, it is still possible for it to become distorted before it is received by the communicatee. What we commonly call noise may very well interfere with the reception of the primary signal. If this happens, the receiver must pick out from this conglomeration of stimuli the ones that the communicator intended for him to receive. This often becomes difficult and, in fact, impossible. You are talking to someone on a street corner, and just as she is replying to your bid for a date that evening, a truck rumbles by, and all you are able to perceive is the movement of her lips—if you happen to be looking at her lips at that specific moment. Many important signals are lost in the noise of a crowd, the shriek of a siren or a clap of thunder. This noise may be much more damaging if it blocks out only enough of the signal so that we feel confident to guess at what the complete signal was.

Discuss several examples of the concept "noise" in the communication process.

The receiver phase of the communication process may also be subject to limitations so that the message it gives to the semantic decoder is not the one initiated by the communicator. Our threshold of reception may play an important part in the way we communicate. This threshold may be the result of some mental activity or of physical impairment. Take the example of the person who moves into a house beside an active railroad. As the 12:02 comes by every night, he is rudely awakened by it for the first few nights, but then, as time goes on some built-in mechanism causes him to be able to sleep right through this noise. Some would say that this is his semantic decoder at work; others would say that his reception level has been raised to the point where he no longer hears this sound. We will not argue this point, but instead, will ask the reader to think of other examples of failures to receive a message, not because of a physical handicap, but because of a mental selection. Those persons who have lost part of their sight or hearing realize only too well the importance of the reception phase of the communication process. If one cannot receive a signal, it is very difficult to react to it.

After one receives a signal, the signal must go through a process of semantic interpretation. We have designated this as semantic decoding. What do the symbols of the code used in this signal mean? How should we react to this particular stimulus? The difference between the semantic encoder and the semantic decoder is that the encoder transforms a specific message into transmittable codes, while the decoder generates an understandable message from the received signal. Thus, the only difference would appear to be in the purpose of the semantic transformation. It should be quite evident to the reader that the semantic decoder is also dependent upon the experience of the individual. The meaning that one person gets from a particular signal may be much different from that which another person gets. We have all too many examples of this in everyday life to fail to see this point.

The response that one makes to a message may be to return a signal to the communicator, in which case the roles of the two are reversed; or he may just decide to store this information in his mind for future reference. In the latter case, where the response is covert rather than overt, the communicator may get only a blank stare as his feedback, and so it may be difficult for him to ascertain what the response really is. Anyone who has lectured to a class at eight o'clock in the morning is very much aware of this phenomenon. We only hope that the reception mechanism is functioning properly and that the material is being stored for future reference.

If we look back at Figure 2 (page 9), we see that it was indicated that the message part of any given communication situation occurs only within the individuals. The reader should realize that the final message resulting from any given situation is a function of the entire process. No one entity can be said to evoke this message, though it may be that one phase of the human-communication process is contributing more interference than are any of the others. We have indicated that interference may occur during any one of the phases. This interference is usually referred to as "noise" in the communication process. The actual noise that is connected with the signal could then be called "noise noise."

Discuss several examples of "noise noise."

Having discussed the various entities of the communication process as depicted by the schema in Figure 3 (page 10), we may now pass on to a further conceptualization of this process. If one takes a more macroscopic view of this process, he sees that it can very well be divided into speaker components (stimulus, semantic encoder, and transmitter), transmission components (transmitter, signal, and receiver), and listener components (receiver, semantic decoder, and response).

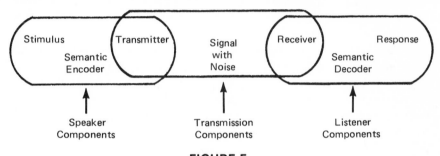

FIGURE 5
A Components Schema

The emphasis of the schema depicted in Figure 3 was on the specific phases occurring in the communication process, while that depicted in Figure 5 is on a way of relating these phases. There have been many books written from both viewpoints. However, it seems that one should carry his conceptualization of these emphases at least one step further.

Again, we may turn to the world of technology to launch us into a new level of insight into the communication process. The following schema is an attempt to illustrate the transformations that take place in a signal from the time it leaves a speaker's mouth until it arrives at the ear of the listener.

In this schema, we have shown seven transformations of the signal into at least four different vehicles for transporting it. The main import of the schema, however, is not the number of transformations nor the number of vehicles used to transport the signal (although these do serve the purpose of letting the reader see just how complicated modern communication networks are). The main import is that each one of the physical entities appearing in Figure 6 acts as both a receiver and as a transmitter. This phenomenon was probably evident in the discussion of the entities of Figure 3. However, the processes depicted in Figure

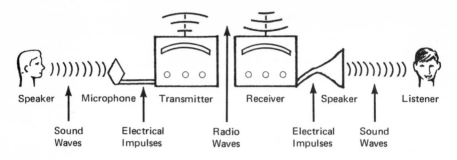

Speaker   ↑   Microphone ↑   Transmitter   Receiver   Speaker   ↑   Listener

| Sound | Electrical | Radio | Electrical | Sound |
| Waves | Impulses | Waves | Impulses | Waves |

FIGURE 6

A Telecommunication Schema

6 make this phenomenon much more perceptible. Notice, for example, that the microphone picks up the sound waves emanating from the speaker's mouth, and in turn, transforms these sound waves into electrical impulses which it sends to the radio transmitter. If one were able to receive electrical impulses as he can receive sound waves, he could "listen in" on the line going from the microphone to the radio transmitter to see if the microphone had made an exact transformation of what the speaker had said. As it is, we must wait until these impulses are transformed back into sound waves before we can make this determination.

This schema illustrates another point in the communication process. The transformations taking place in the network between the microphone and the radio speaker are said to be isomorphic, or at least enough so that sound waves hitting the listener's ears are enough like the sound waves hitting the microphone that the average individual cannot tell them apart.[11] This statement cannot be made about the transformations taking place in the minds of the speaker and the listener. That is, the semantic processes that occur within the speaker and the listener do not permit isomorphic transformations to occur. This is due, of course, to the varying experience of speaker and listener.

The fact that the same entity can be both receiver and transmitter is basic to the concept of communication. It is this fact that makes it difficult to study man as a communicator, since in doing so, one usually truncates the communication process at some point and thus interrupts the continuity of the overall process. Figures 1, 2, 3, and 5 depict the communication process as it occurs between two or more human beings

---

11. An isomorphic transformation means that there is perfect agreement between X before it was transformed into Y and after it is transformed back from Y into X. It is a mathematical concept and not readily applied to psychological concepts. Yet it depicts very well the idealized state of the communication process. If the thoughts that the speaker transforms into speech were the same thoughts evoked in the mind of the listener, then one would say that an isomorphic transformation had occurred.

in one-way communication, that is, the receiver's response is not received by the communicator. In actual communication, the listener's response turns him into the communicator and the communicator into the listener. Thus, one should realize that communication is cyclical and not a one-way process as depicted. In Figure 6 the reader gets his first real glimpse of the fact that one entity may serve both as a receiver and as a transmitter. This brings us to the central theme of this chapter, that is, to look at man as both receiver and transmitter; communicatee and communicator. Taking this view of man allows us to concentrate on the communication process as the natural phenomena occurring within and around each one of us every second of every day that we live.

Perhaps the best way to show how easily one is changed from speaker to listener and vice versa is to superimpose these two schemas.

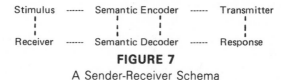

FIGURE 7

A Sender-Receiver Schema

The reader should now be able to see the similarities between these two schemas. One surely must *receive* a *stimulus* to have it play any role in the communication process. Thus, the stimulus and the receiver are very closely related. This is also true of the *transmitter* and the *response.* Any response, even no overt response at all, is transmitted, indicating a close relationship between these two entities.

As for the *semantic encoder* and *decoder,* we have already seen that they both pertain to meaning. Perhaps the only difference between them is the purpose to which they are put. The semantic encoder puts meaning into a code (language or behavior) and the semantic decoder takes meaning out of this code. In both cases it occurs between the reception of a stimulus and the response which we transmit. We may call this intermediate phase the interpretation or information processing phase. Thus, information processing consists of decoding the incoming message and encoding a response to it.

Discuss the similarities and differences between the encoding and decoding processes.

We may subdivide the individual human-communication process into the reception, the processing, and the transmitting of information. This may be depicted by the schema in Figure 8.

Studying man and the communication process from this point of view offers several advantages over the model of Shannon and Weaver. It takes the emphasis off the channel or signal (the mechanical aspect of communication) and places it on the various processes occurring

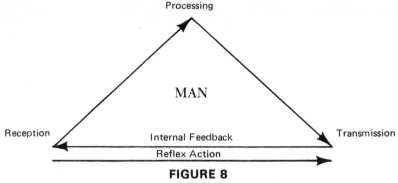

FIGURE 8
The R.P.T. Schema

within the body of man himself. This tends to emphasize the human aspects of communication rather than the technical aspects of a communication system or network (from which the Shannon-Weaver model grew). It still allows one to study the communication process with the message as the cohesive ingredient but from the vantage point of the various phases through which the signal passes while playing its role in the experience of man. This approach puts man and his various abilities at the center of the communication process. It should make one realize that the study of communication is the study of man himself.

Although one can start at any corner of the communication triangle, it would seem to be the most logical to start with reception, go to the processing phase, and then to the transmission phase. The RPT approach allows one to trace the path of a signal from the time it enters the sensory consciousness of a person until this person reacts to the message by transmitting another signal. It should be obvious that man receives his own signals as well as others. Thus, we have indicated the possibility of internal feedback. If one receives a stimulus and responds to it without interpretation, this would be designated a reflex action, such as hitting one's knee and having his lower leg jump.

Discuss the implications of the RPT Model on stimulus-response conditioning.

It is hoped that the RPT approach to communication may help us to recognize the various difficulties that occur in the human-communication process. We must again emphasize that any division of this process is necessarily arbitrary and does not occur in reality, but is a convenient operation for the understanding of the various phases of communication.

It is understood that parts of the reception, processing, and transmission phases are taking place simultaneously and, perhaps, are organically inseparable. However, one looks at each phase as an individual reality because of the convenience it provides for the purposes of theoretical investigation.

If one considers man as the hub of the communication process, then he may interest himself in the various parts of man that are concerned with this process. This interest will lead him to an investigation of the various human activities being studied by many different disciplines in our society. In short, then, one will only understand the human-communication process to the extent that he understands the theories being investigated by the various disciplines active in the study of the many facets of man's behavior. It is hoped that the RPT approach will help the student to see what some of the important areas of research are in this highly complex process.

In taking the RPT approach we are saying that one phase of the communication process is concerned with the collection of data to which the organism may react. This collection of information is carried on via man's senses. By including all of these senses, we are saying that communication may occur as the result of the data gathered by any one or combination of these senses. One might say that they act much like great sponges, soaking up anything and everything in their path. Given these data, man may communicate with his environment; without this information he becomes less than a vegetable. Thus, a very important area of study is that of sensation or sense perception. We should be aware of how the sense organs pick up stimuli and subsequently transform into neurological signals that are transported to the brain.

More than this we should be aware of some of the discoveries being made in neural transmission of information. One should know something about the neurological basis for psychological set and the functioning of various nerve centers in the transmission and modification of information. We should also be familiar with the phenomena called memory. The many studies in both the storage and recall of information are especially relevant to understanding the human-communication process. Memory, of course, allows us to interpret incoming messages against the dimensions of past experiences.

One should also have some understanding of the philosophy and psychology of how our past experiences are associated to form our basic belief and disbelief systems. These systems, functioning as entities which must be kept in balance, seem to be responsible for much of our mental activity. Thus, it is imperative for one who studies the human-communication process, that he be familiar with the various studies delving into the psychological behavior of man. Since this behavior is intimately associated with the cultural and social norms of his environment, to understand man as a communicator, one must know something of the theories being investigated in anthropology and sociology.

The overt behavior of man may be looked upon as the result of the encoding process and as taking the form of both verbal and nonverbal behavior. Therefore, it behooves the human-communication theorist to understand the theories being developed in the areas of speech, linguistics, journalism, mass communication, and human interaction. Couple with this the studies now being done in cybernetics and computer simulation, and it should be evident that for one to understand much of the human-communication process he must have a very broad interdisciplinary background. It is almost as though the study of human communication today infers the study of all the disciplines associated in any way with human behavior, much as rhetoric did in the age of Greece and Rome.

Can you find an academic discipline which is not important to the study of the human-communication process?

What may we conclude, then, about the study of the human-communication process? Perhaps we should conclude by saying that because of the complexity of the communication process and the inability to define human communication to anyone's satisfaction, we might better consider the process itself and study the various phases through which information passes on its way through the human-communication process. Accordingly, whether one considers communication to have taken place when a stimulus activates the central nervous system of a receiver or is more concerned with whether communication may be overt or covert, conscious or unconscious, intentional or unintentional, is of little consequence. Even arguments about what constitutes a message and the controversy over the verbal-nonverbal dichotomy of signals may be viewed in a different light if the RPT approach is taken.

The most important thing is that the student realize that the communication process is a continuing function over time and consequently dependent upon the past experiences and continual interaction of the communicators. In acquiring and disseminating information we know that man must receive it via his senses, store it, process it, and react to it. Thus, any study that helps us understand these and related activities is important to our understanding of the human-communication process. Therefore, a student of human communication should be conversant with the work being done in such academic disciplines as speech, psychology, social-psychology, sociology, anthropology, linguistics, neurology, computer science, philosophy, journalism, and mass media, as well as the technical advances in the clinical treatment of human behavior. Though this seems like a tremendous undertaking, and it is, it is also an extremely rewarding one in terms of personal accomplishment. For the more one understands the human-communication process, the more one understands himself and so may interact more knowledgeably with his fellowman.

In the following chapters we shall survey the basic theories being set forth by researchers in the various disciplines germane to human-communication theory. We shall start with rhetoric and then take up the various theories active in the RPT approach to human communication. Our first purpose will be to discover the principles developed in each theory considered fundamental to a theory of human communication. We shall then discuss some of the more recent theories presented to explain the development of one's communicative behavior.

BIBLIOGRAPHY

1. ARANGUREN, J. L. *Human Communication*. New York: McGraw-Hill Book Company, 1967.
2. BERLO, DAVID K. *The Process of Communication*. New York: Holt, Rinehart and Winston, Inc., 1960.
3. BORDEN, GEORGE A.; GREGG, RICHARD; and GROVE, THEODORE. *Speech Behaviour and Human Interaction*. Englewood Cliffs, N.J.: Prentice-Hall, Inc., 1969.
4. BROWN, ROGER. *Social Psychology*. New York: The Free Press, 1965.
5. CHERRY, COLIN. *On Human Communication*. New York: John Wiley & Sons, Inc., 1957.
6. CONDON, JOHN C., JR. *Semantics and Communication*. New York: The Macmillan Company, 1966.
7. DANCE, FRANK E. X., ed. *Human Communication Theory*. New York: Holt, Rinehart & Winston, Inc., 1967.
8. DUNCAN, HUGH D. *Symbols in Society*. New York: Oxford University Press, 1968.
9. EISENSON, JON J.; AUER, JEFFERY; and IRWIN, JOHN V. *The Psychology of Communication*. New York: Appleton-Century-Crofts, 1963.
10. GRAY, GILES W., and WISE, CLAUDE M. *The Bases of Speech*. New York: Harper & Brothers, Publishers, 1959.
11. HALL, EDWARD T. *The Silent Language*. Greenwich, Conn.: Fawcett Publications, Inc. (a Premier Book d117), 1959.
12. HOVLAND, CARL; JANIS, IRVING; and KELLEY, HAROLD. *Communication and Persuasion*. New Haven: Yale University Press, 1953.
13. MARTIN, HOWARD, and ANDERSEN, KENNETH. *Speech Communication*. Boston: Allyn & Bacon, Inc., 1968.
14. MILLER, GEORGE A. *Language and Communication*. New York: McGraw-Hill Book Company, Inc., 1951.
15. SERENO, KENNETH K., and MORTENSEN, C. DAVID. *Foundations of Communication Theory*. New York: Harper & Row, Publishers, 1970.

16. SHANNON, CLAUDE E., and WEAVER, WARREN. *The Mathematical Theory of Communication.* Urbana: The University of Illinois Press, 1962.

17. SMITH, ALFRED G., ed. *Communication and Culture.* New York: Holt, Rinehart & Winston, 1966.

Chapter 2

THE RHETORICAL TRADITION

It takes very little reflection for one to realize that the way man communicates with man today differs in many ways from the way he communicated centuries ago. A little more reflection reveals that these differences are not all associated with the technological advances of the past centuries. Man has not only reduced distances (telephone, radio, television), improved reception (hearing aids, eye glasses), and augmented memory (printing, recording), but he has also developed a deeper insight into *why* man speaks as he does (psychology, linguistics, psychoanalysis), and *how* man speaks as he does (neurology, physiology, speech pathology), though the latter are dependent on technological advances in other fields.

With our increased understanding of man and his environment, we have also changed our ways of studying man as a communicator. With the advent of new technology and increased educational facilities, man has had to adjust to the "new" ways of communication. This adjustment has affected his approaches to the investigation of human communication, as well as the theories resulting from these investigations. When one looks at the mass of information concerning man as communicator, accumulated over the past 2500 years, the sheer volume tends to inundate us. Yet, contained in this awesome collection of data are most of the principles found in present-day theories of human communication. It would seem relevant, then, to look at our classical heritage and give a brief overview of the development of the rhetorical tradition.

It is common knowledge that man spoke his language long before he wrote it. Thus, it should be expected that man's first interest in the communication process was concerned with oral discourse. Tradition has it that the first organized theory of oral communication was formulated by Teisias or Corax, or both, in the fifth century B.C. in Syracuse, Sicily, to aid in the legal process of property transfer. However, there is evidence to indicate that the ancient Egyptians were aware of the necessity of proper speaking methods much earlier than this.[1] The theories designed to deal with speech were given the general title Rhetoric and were destined to play a major role in the education of schoolboys for 2500 years.

The early Greek civilization relied almost entirely on one's ability to communicate orally for all business transactions. Records began to be kept in writing only after the eighth century B.C. Until that time even history had to be remembered and passed from generation to generation by word of mouth. The poetic form lent itself to this need, but even with this aid to memorization we must compliment the Greeks on their cultivated ability to remember great quantities of information. Formal schooling took about four years after which time the young student was ready to begin the study of speaking, and it was not uncommon for this study to continue for the remainder of his life. The ability to speak well was the most highly prized and sought after accomplishment, and only those who could master the art of speaking could expect to enjoy the respect and admiration of their countrymen.[2]

The oral tradition was so firmly implanted in Greek culture that young people had to learn to speak in public in order to achieve success in life. This, of course, was in the idealized state; not all Greeks achieved the goal of an accomplished public speaker—though this did not diminish the need for this ability. One still had to defend oneself in a court of law or do his own speaking in political argument. This led to the establishment of *logographers*—ghostwriters—one who wrote another man's speech. A man who would employ such a person, and win a case in court on another man's skill, was suspect. Politicians who used logographers tried to keep it a secret, and, in turn, logographers concealed the fact that they were doing this terrible thing as it cast aspersions on their integrity.

Discuss the similarities with today's public speakers and speech writers.

The complete dependence upon public speaking for the Greek citizen led to a desire to know more about the public speaking process. Most schools taught public speaking by imitation, that is, the student watched the master perform and then did as he did. Great emphasis was put on one's ability to reason in a logical manner while thinking on one's feet. The gifted student who mastered this feat invariably became a leader of men. However, as with all educational curriculum, there

---

1. Giles W. Gray, "The 'Precepts of Kagemni and Ptah-Hotep,' " *The Quarterly Journal of Speech,* XXXII (December, 1946), pp. 446-454.
2. See George Kennedy, *The Art of Persuasion in Greece* (Princeton, N.J.: Princeton University Press, 1963), Chapter 1.

were some who objected to the idea that one should be taught to present an argument in a complete package as the orator did. They felt that the ability to probe the depths of knowledge seeking truth was of greater value. Thus, they argued that one who thought he already possessed the truth and so needed only to proclaim it to the masses was deceiving both himself and his audience.

The division between the seekers and the proclaimers is well documented in the dialogues of Plato. Socrates is the ideal seeker, and his opponents, though built up as the ideal orators, were always somewhat inept in their ability to reason. So, as one reads these strange dialogues he finds that Socrates is always able to set up his orator adversary (usually because the orator gives some really inane answers to Socrates' simple questions) and show that he is a man without integrity and very little ability in the reasoning process, which, of course, is the most important human accomplishment. The dialogues are masterfully written and eminently worth one's time to read. Albeit, to the mind of the modern-day student they are apt to soon take on the air of contrived dialogue with Socrates as the all-knowing superman.

What Socrates exemplifies is the masterful art of *Dialectic.* This may be defined as the use of dialogue (questions and answers) to probe a subject and arrive at a greater depth of knowledge than where one began. In this way the proponents of such a method can say that they are seeking the truth. This method, they claim, does away with the bias of the single presentation of what one feels is the truth. What they fail to divulge is that one can ask leading questions and thus bias the development of the final conclusion. This, Socrates did with great skill. Claiming that he knew nothing except the fact that he knew nothing, and that he had an unsatisfiable hunger for truth, he was able to lead his opponents into the most obvious linguistic traps imaginable. The debate over the supremacy of dialectic or rhetoric led eventually to the condemnation and death of Socrates and, perhaps, was the first major indication that man is more concerned with relative than with absolute truth.[3]

Discuss several situations today in which this debate is still a prominent factor.

Dialectic was a thorn in the side of rhetoric. Though rhetoric held a much stronger place in Greek culture, a shrewd dialectician was feared by even the best rhetorician. On the other hand, the rhetorician was the one who was responsible for the progress being made in the development of Greek society. Rhetoric has taken on many definitions over the past 2500 years but originally it meant the art of persuasion

---

3. Plato's Apology, Translated by Benjamin Jowett in *The Dialogues of Plato,* Vol. 7, of the Great Books of the Western World (Chicago: Encyclopaedia Britannica, Inc., 1952), pp. 200-212.

through public speaking. The person who *used* rhetoric was called an orator. The term rhetorician was often used to mean both the theoretician and the user, and in many cases both were one and the same person. However, many times the orator was unaware of the rhetorical principles he was using, and the rhetorician was not always the best speaker.

As Greek society developed, more and more emphasis was placed upon the individual who could persuade an audience. Dialecticians tried to keep the orators honest but this was often neither desirable nor possible. Communication from place to place being very slow, verification of news from another location was often impossible before action was taken on the case at hand. The reliance of the general populace upon the orator for direction in any situation led to the lofty position of power held by those who were glib of tongue. Plato exemplifies the reasonableness of this situation in the dialogue Socrates has with the rhetorician Gorgias. Socrates has been trying to show that since rhetoric has no subject matter it is an evil practice. Gorgias has been trying to show that it is only through the effectiveness of orators (rhetoricians) that progress in any area is made. At one place he says,

> A marvel, indeed, Socrates, if you only knew how rhetoric comprehends and holds under her sway all the inferior arts. Let me offer you a striking example of this. On several occasions I have been with my brother Herodicus or some other physician to see one of his patients, who would not allow the physician to give him medicine, or apply a knife or hot iron to him: and I have persuaded him to do for me what he would not do for the physician just by the use of rhetoric. And I say that if a rhetorician and a physician were to go to any city, and had there to argue in the Ecclesia or any other assembly as to which of them should be elected state-physician, the physician would have no chance; but he who could speak would be chosen if he wished; and in a contest with a man of any other profession the rhetorician more than any one would have the power of getting himself chosen, for he can speak more persuasively to the multitude than any of them, and on any subject. Such is the nature and power of the art of rhetoric! And yet, Socrates, rhetoric should be used like any other competitive art, not against everybody ... the rhetorician ought not to abuse his strength ... for the rhetorician can speak against all men and upon any subject ... in short, he can persuade the multitude better than any other man of anything which he pleases, but he should not therefore seek to defraud the physician or any other artist of his reputation merely because he has the power; he ought to use rhetoric fairly, as he would also use his athletic powers. And if after having become a rhetorician he makes a bad use of his strength and skill, his instructor surely ought not on that account to be held in detestation or banished. For he was intended by his teacher to make a good use of his instructions, but he abuses them. And therefore he is the person who ought to be held in detestation, banished, and put to death, and not his instructor.[4]

It is apparent from the above quote that rhetoric was held in very high esteem by at least part of the Greek civilization. What Gorgias says

4. See Gorgias, in Jowett, *The Dialogues of Plato,* p. 257.

about it is very true. It must be used by *good* people. Bad men might use it to gain their own goals and thus misuse the noble art. They then must be held accountable for their own actions. This led eventually to the definition of an orator as a good man speaking well, and the status of rhetoric as no better than the character of the rhetorician. However, the misuse of rhetoric caused a general distrust of those who were fluent in the spoken word. History has shown that there was good reason for this distrust. The power to persuade is awesome in its potential; frightening in its use. The rise of Adolf Hitler and subsequently World War II are bleak testimony to this power.

Discuss several occupations which depend on the power of persuasion and indicate the level of trust one has for its employees.

In the Greek era much of the significant thinking of the time was done by educators called sophists. They were political activists and very pragmatic in their attempts to attain a specific goal. This led them to argue expediency rather than truth. Because of this, the term sophist soon became associated with those who misused rhetoric. Socrates tried to prove to Gorgias that all rhetoricians were sophists since they were always using whatever means they could muster to arrive at the goal they had set. Gorgias, however, was differentiating between sophists and rhetoricians on the basis of character of the individual under consideration. A rhetorician was a good man with noble goals and undeniable integrity. A sophist was one who was only interested in obtaining the goal set before him—perhaps by his employer. Because of this distinction, anyone who took money to teach rhetoric was suspect, and logographers, who took money and wrote speeches to obtain goals from which they could divorce themselves, were the worst kind. The inability of a listener to tell when a speaker was telling the truth or manipulating evidence to gain desired ends, and the inability to decide whether the speaker was using his own reasoning processes or those of a logographer were so closely tied together that the average citizen began to mistrust all public speakers. This image is still with us today. The art of public speaking is still being taught in much the same way and for much the same purpose as it was in the time of the Greeks. Neither the principles nor the fears have changed to any great extent in these 2500 years.

The possibility of sophistic motives is always present in any communication situation. To cope with these tendencies we may try to know the speaker or the subject better, but we can never be sure we are not being duped. The problem becomes even more severe when we realize that there are times when these techniques are essential to the welfare of humanity. Because of the mental conditions of the audience, the speaker may not be able to use the real facts in the case but may have to revert to other arguments to persuade them to take the necessary action. If this action proves to be best for these people, the speaker is hailed as a great orator (rhetorician); if it proves to be undesirable, he is considered an enemy of the people. A sophist was one who felt that the end justified the means, and the means he used to persuade were not always of the highest ethics. The true rhetorician felt that both the ends and the means had to be of the highest ethical nature.

Discuss several situations where the ends justify any means of persuasion.

This concern over the ethics of persuasion has been a side issue for communication theorists from the earliest times. Certainly those who studied and conceptualized the principles of rhetoric were constantly aware of it. Any new insight into the communication process carried with it the possibility that it might be misused much the same as new insights into nuclear physics carry this possibility today. (And the results may even be as devastating.) We shall return to the ethics of persuasion from time to time as we pursue the theories underlying the understanding of the human-communication process.

The turmoil existing in the Greek mind over dialectic as the method by which one sought out truth, sophistry as the unethical use of persuasive means, and rhetoric as the art of persuasion, led naturally to the development of a body of knowledge concerned with public speaking. As far as we know, it wasn't until Aristotle arrived on the scene in the fourth century B.C. that anyone tried to organize this great body of knowledge into a systematic discipline. As a student of Plato he was very familiar with the dialogues of Socrates, but contrary to Socrates' desire to search for absolute truth, Aristotle chose to organize all existing knowledge. His work in all areas of knowledge is commendable. In the area of rhetoric, very little, if anything new, has been said since his treatise. The reader of Aristotle's *Rhetoric* should continue to bear in mind that oral, face-to-face discourse was the chief means of communication. Aristotle's attempt to systematize this form of discourse may lack some of the psychological refinements of the present day, but it is very thorough in its attempt to analyze public speaking as practiced in his time. Its thoroughness is attested to by the fact that it is still a very fine text for public speaking as practiced today.

Aristotle's insights into the human-communication process were extremely perceptive. It was unfortunate that most of his followers abstracted only certain portions of his insights and expanded them out of all proportion. One aspect of rhetoric which begins to appear in Aristotle's work and develops into a prominent though unseen difficulty for rhetoricians is the supreme position of the signal, that is, the linguistic code into which the message has been put—the speech *per se.* Because most rhetoricians failed to realize the unconscious homage they were paying to the speech itself, they could not shake themselves loose from this burden to allow themselves the freedom of a less biased investigation of the human-communication process. As we shall see, most of their energy was consumed by the analysis of the speech with very little attention paid to human variables.

Aristotle began a very systematic organization of the field of rhetoric.[5] He immediately removed it from the concern of the dialecticians by stating that it is the counterpart of dialectic. In other words, rhetoric is concerned with the proclaiming of the truth, or relative truth, while dialectic is concerned with finding the truth. Having done this he proceeds to explicate the many concerns of rhetoric; the primary concern being the speech itself. A speech is given to present a proof to an audience. In this sense all speeches become persuasive in nature. Therefore, rhetoric was concerned with finding all the available means of persuasion for any given case. One can see, then, how easy it would be to forget about absolute truth and deal with the expediencies of the moment.

Though all speeches were considered to be persuasive, Aristotle was able to classify them into three different types—namely: Deliberative —those dealing with exhortation and concerned with the future and the expediency of developing the correct program; Forensic—those dealing with accusation or defense of past acts and concerned with the meting out of justice; and Epideictic—those dealing with praise or blame and concerned with the present bestowal of honor or dishonor. We are still caught up in the obsession to classify and categorize speeches, though we usually try to divide them into informative, persuasive, and occasional. We have somehow developed the notion that the presentation of information does not persuade, nor does eulogizing or humor.

Discuss the feasibility of differentiating between persuasive and nonpersuasive speeches.

Aristotle's definition indicates that he was more concerned with the means of persuasion than he was with the actual act of speaking. This is further borne out in his desire that the correct methods be used rather than a desire for outward success. It is not strange then to find him stressing to some length the various ways in which one may persuade. Here again he provides us with three categories: Ethos—the image of the speaker, enhanced by his speech, so the audience is persuaded because of the one doing the persuasion; Pathos—involving the listener in an emotional net with the topic so that he is persuaded because of his commitment to an underlying premise; and Logos—the persuasion through direct logical argument. Of these three types of persuasion, ethos is the most potent and, as we shall see, is the most often used in modern times.

5. Lane Cooper, *The Rhetoric of Aristotle* (New York: Appleton-Century-Crofts, Inc., 1932).

When one is required to persuade an audience to do or think something which they would not normally do or think, he must use all the available means of persuasion. Classical rhetoric has categorized some of these means, and we find them just as applicable today as they were in the fifth century B.C. In dealing with the intellect of man, the only time we must persuade him is when the proof of what we are saying is not obvious. Thus, we must use examples to illustrate our points and lines of argument to carry our listeners from the point at which we find them to the point to which we wish them to go. Aristotle called the arguments we use to do this type of persuading enthymemes. Thus, we link fact to fact and arrive at a conclusion that the listener cannot deny if he has agreed with all of our intermediate steps.[6] Add to this the strong use of probabilities and common sense and you have the basis for a powerful theory of persuasion.

Aristotle's theory of rhetoric was very powerful indeed and still represents the major force in the teaching of persuasive speaking. However, one of the major concerns of his theory is being neglected by modern man. Due to the oral nature of all discourse, and the difficulty of writing and carrying notes from which to speak, in ancient Greece, the orator developed another mechanism by which he was able to recall the arguments he wanted to use in his speech. By looking at the various arguments one used in persuading an audience, Aristotle found that these arguments could be categorized into a very few types of arguments. He called these categories TOPOI and lists a great number of them in book two of his treatise on rhetoric. He was able to go even further than just showing that there were various types of arguments; he also found that there were four general topoi being used, namely, arguments that tend to use the principles of more and less, magnifying and minifying, past and future, and possible and impossible.

The idea that arguments tend to cluster into specific types was a prominent part of classical rhetoric. The revival of this idea is due, in part, to the fact that other disciplines have come to recognize the clustering phenomenon in other areas of knowledge. The dimensions of meaning explicated by Osgood[7] and the development of Roget's *Thesaurus* reminded some that not only arguments but knowledge tend to cluster around specific concepts.

This clustering phenomena is being explored by several contemporary theorists, and its relation to the human communication process

---

6. Present day theorists have expanded on the process of argument. The interested reader should see: Stephen Toulmin, *The Uses of Argument* (Cambridge: At the University Press, 1958), and Douglas Ehninger and Wayne Brockriede, *Decision By Debate* (New York: Dodd, Mead & Co., 1963).

7. Charles Osgood, George Suci, and Percy Tannenbaum, *The Measurement of Meaning* (Urbana: The University of Illinois Press, 1957).

noted.[8] If all of one's knowledge is organized around specific topoi, then by employing these we can retrieve all we know about any given subject. This is essentially what we do during the communication process. If we can better understand the use of topoi we may better understand human communication.

Classical rhetorical theory was passed from the Greeks to the Romans where it underwent a process of solidification. As the Greek civilization gave way to the Roman way of life, the centers of education also shifted to that part of the world. Rhetoric seemed to be the main ingredient of the Roman educational system, taking, perhaps, a more important place than it had in the Greek era. With the emphasis on education, the theories of rhetoric were formulated more precisely and its structure solidified. Public speaking was still the main form of mass communication, so that anyone who wanted to advance his station in life had to be able to speak publicly. To obtain this ability the Romans translated the Greek art of rhetoric into their own cultural settings.

Very little happened to rhetoric in its translation from Greek to Latin. Cicero, who was one of the chief orators of the early Roman period (first century B.C.), was also its chief rhetorician. His writings on rhetoric are one of the main sources of information on the nature of early Roman rhetoric. Some of his writings use a dialogue format much like that of Plato, but they lack his liveliness. He also seems to have less philosophical or psychological reasoning behind his system than did Aristotle. Thus, rhetoric begins to take on the appearance of a corpse with rigid, unchangeable rules and regulations. The rigidity of this structure continues to plague rhetoric even to the present day.

The major aspects of rhetorical theory developed in the Roman era were, undoubtedly, the five canons of rhetoric. They were considered to be the essentials for effective public speaking and, if followed, would lead to success. Their universality makes them applicable today and indicates their importance to the human-communication theorist. Although they were developed from considering public speaking as the model, like so many of the rhetorical principles they are also applicable to any communication situation. These five canons cover all aspects of the creation and presentation of verbal discourse.

The first canon, INVENTION, refers to the subject and the appropriate lines of arguments to be used in presenting the subject. The topoi play a major role in this phase of speechmaking; the second canon is

---

8. The interested reader should see: John Wilson and Carroll Arnold, *Public Speaking as a Liberal Art* (Boston: Allyn and Bacon, Inc., 1964); William Nelson, "TOPOI: Evidence of Human Conceptual Behavior," *Philosophy and Rhetoric, II* (No. 1): 1-11; William Nelson, "TOPOI: Functional in Human Recall," *Speech Monographs*, (October, 1970); George Borden and William Nelson, "Toward a Viable Classification Scheme: Some Theoretical Considerations," *American Documentation* (October, 1969), pp. 1-4.

ARRANGEMENT which had to do with the organization of a speech into its several parts as well as the order in which the subject matter was to be given. A speech was thought to consist of an introduction, a body consisting of a narration and proof, and a conclusion. With this overall structure clearly in mind, the speaker must then organize the various arguments he has decided to use in such a way as to elicit the desired response. When this is done he may pass on to the next and third canon, that of STYLE, which was concerned specifically with the words and syntax used in presenting the ideas of the speaker. The fourth canon is MEMORY and was concerned with how the speaker recalled what he wanted to say. It was not the case that they would memorize a speech verbatim, but rather that they would use the topoi as cues to recall the arguments and information they wanted to use. The fifth canon, DELIVERY, was concerned with all the factors involved in the actual presentation of the speech.

Discuss the role of the five canons in your everyday communication situations.

Cicero's explications of rhetoric were the text books for Roman schoolboys for many years. As social and political conditions changed, the emphasis began to move from invention and arrangement to style and delivery. With this change came the relaxing of moral and ethical standards and the rise of sophistry. Public speaking began to be looked upon as a performance much like a theater, where the speaker tried to effect applause for his performance rather than persuasion to a worthy cause. In short, rhetoric and oratory were beginning to look like the entities Socrates had denounced so strenuously five hundred years earlier.

During this time of decay (first century A.D.), Quintilian wrote the most thorough analysis of rhetoric to date. He wrote from the viewpoint that rhetoric was the very core of education. If this premise is true, what type of person should an orator be? Quintilian writes eleven books explaining the role of rhetoric in education and delimiting the various areas of the rhetorical discipline prior to defining what type man the ideal orator should be. Though he feels that the ideal orator is a good man speaking well, he has some difficulty in defining what he means by good. The main thrust of his argument seems to be that he must be a thoroughly educated man so he can make the correct judgment as to what ends he should be striving for. In this respect the ideal orator is more concerned with relative truth than he is with absolute truth, (though his extensive education should have led him to the proximity of absolute truth).

How does one determine the integrity of a speaker? Do the leaders tell the people all they should know? How should censoring be done? What is important news? With our vastly complex society and its mass communication techniques, the problems of ethics increase exponentially. Politicians are accused of telling only what they want the people to know. Advertisers are accused of telling half-truths to sell their products. Yet both of these groups of people are made up of highly educated individuals. Thus, education cannot be the criterion for judging whether an orator is a good man. Quintilian's idealism gives us something to strive for, but like most ideals it is seldom, if ever, reached. Yet in every age there are those orators who stand out as being close to Quintilian's ideal. However, the definition of the word "good" remains a source of contention.

Discuss the ideal orator and give examples.

From the very beginning of the study of public speaking (oratory) man has been confounded by the three horns of rhetoric. Since the study of rhetoric grew out of the need to persuade, the first order of concern was the effect of the public speaker. With results being used as the main criterion for judging the successfulness of a speech, it was natural for sophistry to arise. This led unethical men to preach that the end justifies the means, and for the public to become skeptical of any "good" orator. Thus, the second horn, the ethics of the speaker, was sometimes used as the criterion for the judging of a successful speech. However, after Aristotle systematized the study of rhetoric, man began to look at rhetoric as an art which could be reduced to sets of basic principles. These principles could be taught and one could then judge the success of a speech on how well the speaker employed these principles.[9] This third horn has been the main concern of the rhetoricians.

The oral presentation of information and oral persuasion in a public speaking situation were the main forms of human communication studied by rhetoricians. The development of the five canons gave a well-rounded approach to oratory and are still applicable today. However, the fact remains that the canons which received primary attention were those that were completely focused on the speech *per se.* Indeed, this is probably the most characteristic element of the development of rhetorical theory. The speaker, his audience, and the speech situation were important only in the small effect they might have on the content of the speech. Today we see that most speech texts emphasize these three entities a bit more than the classics, but for the most part the emphasis is still on the formulation of the speech text.

The rhetorician's concern over the content and delivery of a speech led Socrates to rebuke those who practiced this art and denounce them as pure sophists—in the derogatory sense of the word. It also led Quintilian to emphasize the fact that the true orator was one who could not only speak well but was also of reputable character, indicating that a

---

9. Wilson and Arnold, Chapter 12.

good man would not use his art to unworthy ends. As political powers changed in Greece and then Rome, and individual freedoms decreased, the role of rhetoric for the general masses also declined. Fewer and fewer people had the opportunity to achieve success in public speaking for a worthy cause. The major openings for rhetoricians shifted from politics to theater and the emphasis from persuasion to performance. Thus, though Quintilian makes a very strong plea for the elevation of rhetoric to its rightful place in scholarship, one sees that it soon became the art of showmanship and was associated with superficiality and falsehood.

The above characteristics still plague the speech discipline. Very little happened from the third to the seventeenth centuries to help define the role of rhetoric. The elocutionary movement of the seventeenth, eighteenth, and nineteenth centuries only added to the distrust of the general populace for an orator.[10] At the same time, the communication revolution which began in Gutenberg's print shop had engulfed man in one of the most serious problems of his relatively short intellectual history. The fact that man's words could now be reproduced in a mechanical way, which allowed him to speak to masses of people he would never see, gave him new power and new responsibility. The publication of books, magazines, and newspapers (by which we are now being inundated) changed the flow of communication in a very significant manner. Face-to-face communication was reduced to a less significant place in the overall scheme of information dissemination. Printed matter allowed more people to be better informed than ever before.

This, of course, did not happen overnight. In fact, the revolution was so slow and so steady that few realized what was happening. By the time newer methods of communication were invented, man had begun to think in terms of better and faster forms of information dissemination. The impact of commercial publishing added new problems to the rhetorician. He could now get copies of public speeches and consider them in the privacy of his own room, and with the advent of the newspaper a new means of persuasion was realized. Many speeches were made persuasive only by the coverage they were given in the newspapers. Masses were able to "hear" what important people had to say by reading their newspapers. But reading a speech to yourself is far different than hearing someone give it. Thus, you should be able to see some of the implications of mass communication.[11]

---

10. See Karl Wallace, ed., *History of Speech Education in America* (New York: Appleton-Century-Crofts, Inc., 1954).

11. Wilbur Schramm, *Responsibility in Mass Communication* (New York: Harper & Brothers, 1957).

Discuss some of the differences between reading and hearing a speech.
One need only think for a few minutes on this subject to realize that many problems have faced man since he has gained this tremendous ability to communicate to the masses. The predominant two-way communication situation of face-to-face communication gave way to the one-way communication situation of a mechanical society. What effect did the lack of immediate feedback have on the human-communication process? This is one question that few, if any, researchers have investigated. Yet one cannot pass it off lightly just because its emergence was so slow that no one recognized it until it became a way of life. The problems associated with this lack of feedback are found in all the censorship questions we are facing today. Man no longer has the freedom to choose what information he will receive into his cognitive system. This is a very important problem in understanding the human-communication process.

Discuss the role of personal responsibility in the communication situations involving dialectic, rhetoric, and mass communication.

Summary:

In this chapter we have tried to present the highlights of our rhetorical tradition. We have seen how rhetoric developed in the face of dialectic, sophistry, and elocution. In the process of this development, we have seen that many worthwhile concepts were developed and passed on to other disciplines: Some of these concepts are the intentions of the communicator—which play a major role in the definitions of dialectic, rhetoric, and sophistry; the concepts of ethos, pathos, and logos as forms of proof and thus means of persuasion; the concepts of Topoi and enthymeme as ingredients in the reasoning process; the five canons—invention, arrangement, style, memory, and delivery—as phases of the rhetorical process; and the concept of ethics or responsibility as a basic consideration for every rhetorical act. All of these concepts have their place in the theory of human communication. Thus the reader is urged to obtain a sound foundation in rhetoric before he attempts to develop a theory of human communication.

BIBLIOGRAPHY

1. BAIRD, A. CRAIG. *Rhetoric: A Philosophical Inquiry.* New York: The Ronald Press Co., 1965.

2. BALDWIN, CHARLES. *Ancient Rhetoric and Poetic.* Gloucester, Mass.: Peter Smith, 1959.

3. ———, *Medieval Rhetoric and Poetic.* Gloucester, Mass.: Peter Smith, 1959.

4. ———, *Renaissance Literary Theory and Practice.* Gloucester, Mass.: Peter Smith, 1959.

5. BLACK, EDWIN. *Rhetorical Criticism.* New York: The Macmillan Co., 1965.

6. BLAIR, HUGH. *Lectures on Rhetoric and Belles Lettres.* Carbondale: Southern Illinois University Press, 1965.

7. BRYANT, DONALD, ed. *The Rhetorical Idiom.* Ithaca, N.Y.: The Cornell University Press, 1958.

8. CAMPBELL, GEORGE. *The Philosophy of Rhetoric.* Carbondale: Southern Illinois University Press, 1963.

9. CLARK, D. L. *Rhetoric in Greco-Roman Education.* New York: Columbia University Press, 1957.

10. CLARKE, M. L. *Rhetoric at Rome.* New York: Barnes & Noble, Inc., 1963.

11. COOPER, LANE. *The Rhetoric of Aristotle.* New York: Appleton-Century-Crofts, Inc., 1932.

12. CORBETT, EDWARD. *Classical Rhetoric for the Modern Student.* New York: Oxford University Press, 1965.

13. KENNEDY, GEORGE. *The Art of Persuasion in Greece.* Princeton: Princeton University Press, 1963.

14. NICHOLS, MARIE HOCHMUTH. *Rhetoric and Criticism.* Baton Rouge: Louisiana State University Press, 1963.

15. RICHARDS, I. A. *The Philosophy of Rhetoric.* New York: Oxford University Press, 1965.

16. SCHWARTZ, JOSEPH, and RYCENGA, JOHN. *The Province of Rhetoric.* New York: The Ronald Press Co., 1965.

17. SMITH, JAMES, and PARKS, E. W. *The Great Critics.* New York: W. W. Norton & Co., 1951.

18. THONSSEN, LESTER, and BAIRD, A. CRAIG. *Speech Criticism.* New York: The Ronald Press Co., 1948.

19. WALLACE, KARL, ed. *History of Speech Education in America.* New York: Appleton-Century-Crofts, Inc., 1954.

20. WHATELY, RICHARD. *Elements of Rhetoric.* Carbondale: Southern Illinois University Press, 1963.

21. WILSON, JOHN, and ARNOLD, CARROLL. *Public Speaking as a Liberal Art.* Boston: Allyn & Bacon, Inc., 1964.

Chapter 3

SOME
PSYCHONEUROLOGICAL
CONSIDERATIONS

In the foregoing chapter we were concerned with man's approach to the communication process up to the twentieth century. This approach has been primarily through the discipline rhetoric, and has been concerned primarily with the communiqué rather than the communicants. During the seventeenth, eighteenth, and nineteenth centuries the focus of concern began to shift from the speeches to the speakers. This is seen in both the formal rhetorical theories, which began to adopt the fledgling psychological theories to explain the effects of public speaking, and the elocutionist's theories, which tried to prescribe how a *person* should deliver various types of speeches.

By the turn of the twentieth century scholars were beginning to think in terms of individual behavior, though they had not really connected this with communication theory. Scientific sophistication was creeping into the disciplines of psychology and sociology, and an acceptable body of knowledge was being compiled. The rhetorical factions merged with the elocutionary factions and formed the discipline called speech. This discipline maintained the most valuable assets of both these factions, that is, the synthesizing nature of their research, but was also saddled with the most damaging of their reputations, namely, sophistry. So, although the speech discipline was doing some good work in the area of human communication, it was not being accepted by the rest of the academic world because of its reputation.

Because of the above situation, most of the progress in the study of the human-communication process is attributed to the disciplines of psychology, sociology, and linguistics. A notable example of this is the work of the Yale teams organized around Carl Hovland (a psychologist) and producing *The Yale Studies in Attitude and Communication.* This series of studies begins with the traditional rhetorical approach (looking at the effects of communiqués) and works itself back into the psychological underpinnings of attitude change. Psychologists have continued to work in this area of attitude change and communicative behavior especially in their branch called social psychology. It may be interesting to note that this branch purports to be an amalgamation of sociology and psychology in which its adherents synthesize the information from both parent disciplines into a theory of man's social behavior.

The speech discipline has attempted to do much more than the above. We attempted to synthesize information from every pertinent field into a theory of how and why man communicates the way he does. We have moved slowly from the prescriptive exercises of the past to the descriptive exercises of the present. In our attempts to describe the communication process we have called on all major disciplines to add their knowledge to this very complex project. Being good rhetoricians we have used all available means to accomplish this task. Our research methods encompass all the approaches to data gathering. At the same time we have been very slow to move away from the traditional approach of using the speech *per se* as our independent variable. Perhaps it is because of this that we have been unable, until recently, to see that the immediate linguistic signal (the speech) is only a small part of the overall communication process. In the following pages an attempt will be made to bring many of the "outside" disciplines to bear on the study of the human-communication process.

Since we were concerned primarily with the speech in the last chapter, perhaps we should begin with this aspect of the communication process. We used the following schema to define the communication process.

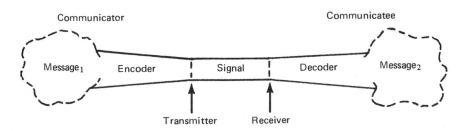

FIGURE 9

A Communication Schema

It should be obvious that this is a flip-flop model, meaning that in two-way communication the communicator and the communicatee are constantly changing places. It should also be noted that what we have traditionally called the message is now called a signal, since the message (being equated with meaning) only occurs in the minds of the communicants. Thus a rhetorical critic becomes a verbal signal analyzer, while a human-communication theorist tries to isolate all of the signals passing between communicants, both verbal and nonverbal, and to ascertain what part each plays in evoking the message generated in the mind of the receiver.

Discuss the intricacies of the seven elements of the above model and the flip-flop notion.

As was pointed out in the last chapter, the rhetorician has been very concerned with the verbal signal and how it evokes meaning in the mind of the receiver. Present-day evidence points to the fact that there is much more than language working in the communication process. Two men, Vance Packard and Marshall McLuhan, have been publicized as the leaders of the present multidimensional approach to the human-communication process. Though the percepts of both these men have been known for many years, it took a concerted effect by ad men to make this general knowledge. This in itself is a commentary on our knowledge of the communication process.

Though we have tried to chide rhetoric for being overly concerned with the signal in a communicative situation, it wasn't until the twentieth century that man discovered that any innovation he instigated in the communicative process carries a message of its own. If one defines signal as any stimulus which affects man's behavior, then every technological invention man has made to augment the human-communication process is a signal itself. We have already seen how technical advances brought with them many ethical questions. Now we would like to see what the technical advances said apart from their content.

Perhaps the easiest way to see that new innovations evoked a message themselves is to look at cross-cultural studies. The differences between advanced and primitive cultures are nearly always their technological advances. If an African bushman could be placed in the United States instantaneously, all of his senses would suddenly be bombarded with many new stimuli. His mental capacity would be strained to accept and assimilate these stimuli into his intellectual framework. His past experiences would be of little help in explaining the world around him. It is our communicative capacity (both as an encoder and a decoder of messages) that structures our view of reality, and any innovation in the structure of the world around us evokes a message to our intellect to change its view of reality.

We have now broadened the idea of message producing signals to include all stimuli that affect our view of reality. As we expand on the meaning of communication you may find that you cannot include all that we take in under this rubric. However, the mere fact that you have been subjected to this conceptual barrage will enhance the learning process and broaden your view of reality. This is precisely the case in point. Any change in our environment affects the way we see the world. It changes our desires, our expectations, and our fears. Therefore, we are a different people than we were before this environmental change. Thus, communication has occurred.

Discuss various environmental changes and the ways in which they have changed your views of the world.

The "medium is the message"[1] is the oft-quoted line of Marshall McLuhan which has shaped the thinking of many in the field of human-communication theory. His explanation of the idea that every techno-logical advance is but an extension of some part of man has raised many questions and served as a stimulus for many profitable discussions of the communication process. What does it all mean? We have mentioned the fact that our environment affects our world view. It should be easy to go one step further and see that if technological advances help us to interact with our environment in new and more precise ways, then they become extensions of ourselves. At the same time, since they now form part of our environment they evoke messages in and of them-selves.

What is the effect of man's extension of himself? As we mentioned before, man is a social animal. The essence of his life seems to be his interaction with other human beings. This means that his ability to communicate is the most important facet of his entire being. When he extends himself through his technological advances, he is increasing his potential for communication. Developments in transportation and communication media have made the world his playground. Whereas, in pretechnological times he was concerned with only his immediate family and their welfare within the few miles he could traverse, he must now be concerned with the welfare of millions of others because they are as close as his television set. The intimacy with which we see the world has brought Shakespeare's stage into our living room. At the same time we are still trying to live as we did in the pretechnological days in both social and political dimensions.

Our ability to accept and interpret information has changed very little over the past two thousand years. Yet the amount of information that we must process has doubled and tripled so many times it is impos-sible to compare our present information load with that of even a few centuries ago. Our senses are continually bombarded with signals beg-ging to be interpreted and stored in our information bank. We have become so enveloped in this information maze that our mind refuses to admit receiving even half of the information fed into it. This is evidenced by the increasing number of witnessed crimes being com-

---

1. Marshall McLuhan, *Understanding Media: The Extensions of Man* (New York: McGraw-Hill Book Company, 1964).

mitted each day. We have become passive about most of the things that others say we should be concerned about because we just cannot accept any more information into our active processing module.

What happens when our brain becomes overloaded with information to be processed? Dr. James G. Miller has spent much time in attempting to solve this question. In one series of experiments he tried to measure the effects of overload on five levels of systems. He started with the single nerve cell of a frog.

> The frog's nerve cell was fed bits of "information" in the form of electric pulses of increasing frequency. The cell's output, or the rate at which it "fired," was measured. Up to about 4,000 bits per second, the cell's output kept up with its input. Then the output leveled off and refused to go higher, and as the input rate was stepped up, the output began to fall off, ending far below 4,000 bits per second.

> Moving up from the level of one cell to the level of an organ, the Michigan group tested the visual pathway of a rat. The optic nerve was stimulated electrically and the pathway's output measured. The group of nerve cells showed the same performance pattern as the single cell, except that the peak capacity was only 55 bits per second, compared to 4,000 for the single cell.

> Next, a human was put to work pushing a button in time to a variably blinking light. Again came the same pattern of rising output with rising input, then a decline in performance as input continued to increase. And the maximum capacity was only five or six bits per second.

> When the blinking-light experiment was performed with two people transmitting signals to a third, the peak "channel capacity" was about 3 1/2 bits per second. With the signals passing through three echelons of three people, peak capacity was 2 1/2 bits per second.

> In other words, as a system or channel becomes more complex, its capacity drops. And always its output rate falls when it is overloaded with more bits of information than it can handle.[2]

Hermann draws the conclusion, "When an electrical circuit is overloaded with more current than it can carry, it burns out or blows a fuse. And when a man, such as an overworked executive, is regularly loaded with more information than he can 'process,' he too may blow a fuse."[3] But what does it mean to "blow a fuse"? Our mental hospitals and psychiatric clinics are filled with patients suffering from information overload. And it would appear that this is only a minor part of the affected group. Doctors now say that it is the chief cause of ulcers, high blood pressure, hypertension, and heart attack. It would appear, then, that man's extension of himself has not been very beneficial to the individual's information processing system. However, since we have to accept this continued technological acceleration as a way of life, it

2. Robert Hermann reports this in his column, "Does a Human, Pressured, Really 'Blow a Fuse'?" *The National Observer,* Vol. 4, No. 1, Monday (January 4, 1965) p. 12.
3. Ibid., p. 1.

would appear that we should be interested in understanding its implications so we could better cope with it. This is one area of research for the communication theorist.

Discuss ways in which one can cope with man's continued extension of himself.

Now we must move on to another level of difficulty. It is one thing to know how to cope with an information overload; it is another to know when it occurs. We have all grown up in a world in which the rate of change, in terms of the extensions of man, has continually increased. All of us have accepted this notion of change—indeed we expect it. On the other hand, it is difficult for us to realize what it would be like to live in a society in which our "way of life" is not *the* way of life. This is attested to by the fact that our Peace Corps volunteers must go through an elaborate conditioning period before they are sent out to another culture. Once there, they usually adapt quite readily to the environment. However, it seems to be much easier to go down the cultural ladder than to move up, for when these same young people return to the United States, they often find it more difficult to adapt to this environment than to more primitive cultures—even though they had lived here before. The information overload hitting them when they came back to our society—in just sheer noise and superfluous information—is overwhelming.

One is inclined to wonder why we are not able to control the reception of information which our brain must interpret. We usually take pride in the fact that we are living in the age of existentialism and thus masters of our own fate. A quick look around us should make us aware that this is not the case at all. One of the greatest industries of the modern world thrives on the fact that we can be controlled by forces of which we are not aware. Advertising psychology has developed to the extent that marketers are constantly catching us off guard. As soon as one ploy has been uncovered, two new ones take its place, and even though we have become very skeptical of advertisements, we are still highly influenced by them.

Man's inability to understand what makes him behave the way he does is a legitimate area of concern for those interested in the human-communication process. The fact that man's senses are continually battered by signals of one kind or another means that he should be aware of the effects of these signals and whether or not he accepts them on a conscious level. The mere thought that man can be influenced on a subconscious level suggests all kinds of evil and devious means of influencing his behavior. Therefore, all of us should be aware of the fact that we are affected subconsciously by the signals we receive.

Vance Packard's classic example of the strength of soap detergents points out our vulnerability.

The Color Research Institute had what it felt was a startling encounter with this proneness to irrationality when it tested package designs for a new detergent. It was testing to see if a woman is influenced more than she realizes, in her opinion of a product, by the package. It gave the housewives three different boxes filled with detergent and requested that they try them all out for a few weeks and then report which was the best for delicate clothing. The wives were given the impression that they had been given three different types of detergent. Actually only the boxes were different; the detergents inside were identical.

The design for one was predominantly yellow. The yellow in the test was used because some merchandisers were convinced that yellow was the best color for store shelves because it has very strong visual impact. Another box was predominantly blue without any yellow in it; and the third box was blue but with splashes of yellow.

In their reports the housewives stated that the detergent in the brilliant yellow box was too strong; it even allegedly ruined their clothes in some cases. As for the detergent in the predominantly blue box, the wives complained in many cases that it left their clothes dirty looking. The third box, which contained what the institute felt was an ideal balance of colors in the package design, overwhelmingly received favorable responses. The women used such words as "fine" and "wonderful" in describing the effect the detergent in that box had on their clothes.[4]

There are other forms of manipulation which have proved successful. The use of subliminal perception gained some publicity a few years ago when advertisers were allowed to insert short ads like "popcorn" or "Coca-Cola" into a regular movie film in such a way that the eye could not consciously detect it. They found out that the behavior of the audience was significantly altered toward the purchasing of such products. The implications of such behavior made them outlaw this type of advertising. Yet this shows quite clearly that we can be manipulated by those things we are unaware of.

What controls our behavior? Are we really aware of what we perceive? What effect does the behavior of others have on our own behavior? These questions keep pressing us on toward the goal of understanding all human behavior. However, since human behavior is not always rational to the one observing it, how can we know what provoked this behavior? The answer is, we cannot. There is evidence that we cannot even be sure we have isolated the right clues to observe. For example: fluency in public speaking has long been equated with one's ability to put one word after another in continuous discourse without observable auditory pauses. However, experimental evidence claims that the cues for our perception of fluency are picked up from the nonverbal behavior of the speaker rather than his verbal behavior.[5]

---

4. Vance Packard, *The Hidden Persuaders* (New York: David McKay Company, Inc. 1957), pp. 16-17. Copyright © 1957 by Vance Packard. Reprinted by permission of the publishers, David McKay Company, Inc.

5. Milton Horowitz, "Fluency: An Appraisal and a Research Approach," *The Journal of Communication* (March, 1965), pp. 4-13.

There are other areas of gross misunderstandings about our knowledge of ourselves. It was long thought that we could be trusted to say what we meant; at least when asked what we wanted. Yet the Edsel fiasco is proof that when the producers comply with what the people say they want, this does not satisfy them. Our linguistic behavior is often in contradiction to our nonverbal behavior. When we begin to think of all the variables that are active in our decision-making processes we begin to see how complicated the process really is. Not only are we affected by our own beliefs and desires but also by those of our peer groups and our immediate associates. It is very seldom, if ever, that we can say we made a decision without having its effect on others affect this decision.

Perhaps the most observable use of manipulation was that of the German people by Adolf Hitler in the 1930's. He was able to use mass persuasion in its grandest manner to accomplish the most abhorrent spectacle modern man has had to witness. His use of propaganda through the existing media and the psychology of situations was superb from a technological point of view. Today we would call it brainwashing, but regardless of what it is called, it accomplished the end—of convincing a nation that it was invincible and right in what it was doing. Neither could be further from the truth. But what does the example of Hitler tell us about the accessibility of the mind of an audience? Primarily, it says that we are vulnerable to manipulation. It would seem that the only way we can combat this manipulation is to be educated to its existence and to an awareness of the variables active in human communication.

Discuss the differences between manipulation and persuasion and the ethics involved in each.

Since we are not always aware of what is going on in the human-communication process, is there any way we can collect more and better evidence from which to build theories?

Much of the behavioral research of the twentieth century has been intimately concerned with the measurement of various aspects of the human-communication process. The methods developed have generally fallen into two distinct categories, namely, psychological and physiological. Both have been predicated on the stimulus-response model. Thus, if a person receives a communiqué, he is bound to react to it. The measuring devices attempt to quantify the resulting behavior for purposes of analysis.

All measuring devices claim success far beyond their actual capabilities. The most reasonable conclusion one can draw is that for a given purpose a particular test does as well as can be expected given our present degree of knowledge. However, the importance of these measuring instruments cannot be cast off so lightly, for if man can quantify his communicative behavior he should be able to understand it better. As more knowledge accrues, better tests are developed. One may never settle the dispute between the advocates of psychological and physiological measurements, but one can develop finer and more reliable instruments.

It should be obvious why a person interested in studying the human-communication process should concern himself with various types of measuring instruments. The answer should be apparent from the last few pages. It is good to be able to identify communication situations from empirical data; it is better to be able to extract from these happenings a theory about how and why they occur; but it is best to be able to quantify the variables active in the situation for further experimentation, validation, and analysis. The quantification of communicative behavior allows for objective analysis resulting in verifiable hypotheses. Thus, the desire to obtain such data continually pushes man to greater efforts in the development of reliable measuring instruments.

Occasionally the development of a measuring device will help to illuminate a particular part of the human-communication process. Such is the case with the pupil dilation studies of Eckhard Hess.[6] These studies have given concrete verification to assumptions made centuries ago—that nonverbal stimuli are significant factors in the human-communication process. It illuminates many aspects of subconscious communication by revealing our subconscious reactions to incoming stimuli. Thus, it not only validates many of the theories about the human-communication process but also gives researchers a more subtle way to measure reactions to incoming signals. The implications of this research are many. The questions it raises are even more.

According to Hess's theory, the pupils of the eyes dilate when one's brain is actively engaged in processing information. Thus, pupil dilation may show interest in a stimulus, activity during problem solving, or (perhaps) pleasurable daydreaming. The latter has not been experimentally verified, though it follows from the information that is now available. Pleasurable experiences cause the pupils to dilate; painful stimuli cause them to constrict. Expert card sharks and oriental traders use this uncontrollable response to tell them how well they are doing. Of course, there are other nonverbal reactions that may be "read" as well, but to get an idea of how reliable a measurement this is, try showing various pictures to a friend and see which ones produce the pupil dilation. But be careful, it has also been known to reveal homosexual tendencies.[7]

---

6. From Eckhard Hess, "Attitude and Pupil Size," *Scientific American* (April, 1965), pp. 46-54. Copyright © 1965 by *Scientific American, Inc.* All rights reserved.

7. Eckhard Hess, "Pupils Response of Hetero and Homosexual Males to Pictures of Men and Women," *Journal of Abnormal Psychology,* Vol. 7, 1965.

Work in pupil dilation has also revealed that the receiver is not always aware of what it is that has given him a pleasurable experience. Hess gives the following experimental evidence.

> One of the most interesting things about the changes in pupil size is that they are extremely sensitive, sometimes revealing different responses to stimuli that at the verbal level seem to the person being tested quite similar. We once demonstrated this effect with a pair of stimulus photographs that in themselves provided an interesting illustration of the relation between pupil size and personality. In a series of pictures shown to a group of 20 men we included two photographs of an attractive young woman. These two slides were identical except for the fact that one had been retouched to make the woman's pupils extra large and the other to make them very small. The average response to the picture with the large pupils was more than twice as strong as the response to the one with small pupils; nevertheless, when the men were questioned after the experimental session, most of them reported that the two pictures were identical. Some did say that one was "more feminine" or "prettier" or "softer." None noticed that one had larger pupils than the other. In fact, they had to be shown the difference. As long ago as the Middle Ages women dilated their pupils with the drug belladonna (which means "beautiful woman" in Italian). Clearly large pupils are attractive to men, but the response to them—at least in our subjects—is apparently at a nonverbal level. One might hazard a guess that what is appealing about large pupils in a woman is that they imply extraordinary interest in the man she is with![8]

Are you a pupil watcher? Think of the many ways women are attracting you with their eyes. Is it possible for you to control the dilation of your pupils? There are many interesting questions that arise from this aspect of the human-communication process.

If pupil dilation is an accurate measure of mental activity, is it possible to interpret the correct meaning of pupil dilation?

The above information on the subtleness of our perceptions leads us to wonder about the ways in which we are affected by our environment. Can we isolate any of the variables that are dominant in affecting our cognitive activity? Some work has been done to show that one aspect of the environment which influences us is the exposure we have to a stimulus. Just exposure alone may account for many of our attitude changes.[9] On meeting a person for the first time you may have misgivings about him, but after you have seen him several times your attitude often changes to one of liking the individual. People are often changed from our like to our dislike category after we "get to know them." There has been a lot said about first impressions and "keeping one's mouth shut" so as not to confound a good physical image. However, though much of our attitude change is due to learning more about a person, much can also be accomplished by mere exposure to, or the awareness of, the existence of the person.

8. Eckhard Hess, "Attitude and Pupil Size," p. 50.
9. See Robert Zajonc, "Attitudinal Effects of Mere Exposure," *Journal of Personality & Social Psychology* (1968): 9(2, pt. 2), pp. 1-27.

What happens when we encounter a new stimulus for the first time? The circumstances of the encounter will have a great effect on the resulting attitude we form toward the source of the stimulus. If our attitude is not negative, then repeated exposure to this stimulus will insure a favorable attitude toward its source. This is true of words as well as humans or inanimate objects. It is not at all clear how negative attitudes are produced, but repeated exposure to an already negatively perceived object will only increase this unfavorable attitude. It is only when one is repeatedly exposed to an unfamiliar stimulus that the favorable attitude develops.

What does this mean in terms of a theory of human communication? First, we must realize that the individual's personality plays a major role in whether he perceives a stimulus negatively or positively. Our basic approach to life is the psychological set within which we interpret each stimulus. Our psyche appears to require some pre-formed expectation for every event that affects it. When this information is not available to it, it enters the experience with varying degrees of uncertainty. But this uncertainty must be resolved and most people tend to resolve it toward the favorable end of the continuum if they do not receive any unfavorable information about the stimulus. Repeated exposure to the stimulus makes it familiar, and familiarity is apparently a positive feeling.

Little evidence is available to enlighten us on the effect of exposure to stimuli about which we have strong feelings. It does seem plausible from effects of campaign rhetoric to say that exposure to a name or an issue even in the negative vein will affect positively those persons who are not committed negatively to the name or issue. It could also be assumed that continued exposure to a pleasurable stimuli, if not overexposed, would bring about continued reinforcement of this positive attitude. What does this say about our advertising theories? Going on the assumption that one must attract the public to one's product, to expose him to this product they are using more and more sex-oriented ads. These ads draw attention to *both* products being displayed, and it is not at all clear which product is gaining more *consumers* from this exposure.

Discuss the implications of the exposure theory in relation to television.

It should now be clear that man is not always aware of what is communicating to him nor how this communication takes place. Present-day attempts to erase this uncertainty are taking the shape of intimate studies of man himself. Of course, man can be studied on many different levels: neurologically, physiologically, psychologically, sociologically, and philosophically. All of the approaches to the study of man help him to understand himself better, and since each approach attacks the problem in a different manner, it is imperative that the student of human communication be aware of these approaches. Though the majority of studies concerned with man as a communicator seem to be in the area of theory building around abstract concepts, many of the important advances in the understanding of man as communicator are coming from the area of study concerned with the physiological basis of behavior.

In the preceding pages we were concerned with the way man behaved and the attempts at influencing this behavior. Now we would like to point out some of the neurological bases for this behavior. We know that when a stimulus is received by man it is done so by the five senses. These sense organs then transform this signal into a code that can be carried by our nervous system to the brain and interpreted there. If one understands a little about the workings of this system, he will have a better basis for the understanding of the human-communication process. This knowledge should give him some understanding of why communication can be as complicated as it is.

We need say very little about the sense organs. You have learned about them since you were in grade school. To put your knowledge into our frame of reference, however, we should mention that each sense organ is unique, in that it will receive only one type signal, and that the external signal goes no further than the sense organ. When a signal is received by any of these sense organs it is transformed into a series of neurological impulses and sent on its way to the brain. Thus our sense organs are really only transformers used to convert external signals into internal signals. They have a short memory of the signal received and, unless they are impaired, send a complete reproduction of this signal to the brain. Their function, then, is to collect information, transform it into neurological impulses, and transmit it to the brain.

The neurological impulses which travel to the brain from the sense organs appear to be very similar when recorded on an oscilloscope. It has been found that as they travel along the central nervous system to the brain they may be modified or blocked by counter neurological action. Each nerve cell acts as a booster station and when it transmits a signal sends it out with the same characteristics as it came in with. Thus the signal does not die out from lack of energy. However, this signal may be blocked by other neurological impulses. This is accomplished by raising the firing threshold of the cell so that the incoming signal is not of sufficient strength to cause the cell to fire and send the signal on to the brain. Since a message is generated from a series of neuronal impulses, a blocking of any of these impulses will cause the message generated to be altered from the intended message. Most of these inhibitory signals are sent out by the brain though some of them may originate with the sense organs.

Besides the fact that the central nervous system can block neuronal signals and thus control the resultant message, there is another facet of this system which affects the communication process. The reticular formation serves as a control center for the activity of the brain. When a neuronal signal approaches the brain it is first evaluated by the reticular formation, and, if it finds the signal "important," it will arouse the brain to receive the signal. If the brain is not aroused the signal is not processed by it. It is assumed that this control center has an active part in our focus of attention and is intimately involved in the effect of drugs. As the high command of our central nervous system it functions to keep us "tuned in" on both external and internal signals.

The ability of the central nervous system to affect the signals being transmitted to the brain has many implications for the human-communication process.[10] We cannot be sure that the signals received by the sense organs are ever interpreted by the brain. If their internal code is modified before it gets to the brain, then the message evoked cannot be the one intended by the communicator.[11] Thus we find a neurological basis for psychological set, and we can understand why some people act as though they do not see the world in the same way we do. If the brain receives signals not intended by the communicator, then there is a great deal of room for trouble in the communication process. This possibility of trouble is magnified when we realize that it is our own brain that may have altered the incoming signals. The communication theorist should be aware of these neurological phenomena.

Discuss the implications of the fact that the central nervous system is able to control the functioning of its parts.

When the signals reach the brain they must be stored for future use. Probably the most important and the best hidden secret of man is his memory. This thing which is sometimes an abstract concept, sometimes a physiological reality, has baffled researchers for centuries. It seems that one is not really sure what it is nor how it is accomplished. Yet for man to communicate it is absolutely essential that he has a memory. The very core of all intellectual enterprises is intimately involved with what we call memory. Learning, thought, creativity, speaking, understanding, and so forth, are dependent on the ability to remember. However, the preceding two sentences depict a duality of this phenomena which few people realize exists yet with which everyone is familiar.

The two basic problems which arise in verbal communication (the form of communication which uses words as the vehicle) are having

---

10. See a review of these implications in George Borden, Richard Gregg, and Theodore Grove, *Speech Behavior and Human Interaction* (Englewood Cliffs: Prentice-Hall, Inc., 1969); also the interested student may want to read more indepth analyses of these neurological phenomena in the following articles in *Scientific American*. Sir John Eccles, "The Synapse" (January, 1965), pp. 56-66; J. D. French, "The Reticular Formation" (May, 1957); Bernhard Katz, "How Cells Communicate" (September, 1961); Ronald Melzack, "The Perception of Pain" (February, 1961); and William Miller, et. al., "How Cells Receive Stimuli," (September, 1961).

11. George A. Borden, "Mathematical Transformations and Communication Theory," *The Journal of Communication* (June, 1963), pp. 87-93.

something to say and being able to recall the words in which to phrase it. One sometimes finds himself in the philosophical argument as to whether one who cannot say it linguistically really has anything to say. (Is all meaning verbal?) Regardless of how this argument ends, one is sure to realize that a person who is glib has a very efficient verbal recall mechanism, even though he may be using his full linguistic capacity. On the other hand, a very brilliant person may not be able to convey his ideas well because he lacks the ability to recall the correct language rapidly enough to make a fluent statement.

A little reflection (which involves memory) should make you aware of how important memory is to the human-communication process. It is only a short step from there to asking what are today's researchers finding out about memory? How far have we come toward solving the riddle of the neurological basis for memory? Psychologists, neurologists, and physiologists are making great strides in their attempt to break the riddle of memory. Biochemists have now stepped into the arena and are looking for the basic building blocks of memory. To get the latest results of all of these efforts to solve this mystery the reader should read about it in the current volume of *The Annual Review of Psychology.* Having done this he will realize that several promising leads are being followed to unravel this mystery.

The latest theories about memory say that memory is a system involving the elements DNA, RNA, protein, and sugar. This all began with the discovery of the DNA molecule.[12] Space does not allow us to give a complete review of the theories involved in this research, but the reader should understand that this research is primarily concerned with the storage of material. If we can find out how information is stored in the brain, then we can begin to work on the problem of the recall of this information. Although it is necessary for one to have the information in his memory before he can communicate it, it is the recall phase of memory that is of primary interest to the communication theorist. He may base his theories on either the assumption that every impulse reaching the brain is stored or on the assumption that the brain exercises selective storage of information. In either case, the human-communication theorist's main concern is how the information stored in the brain is recalled and utilized in the communication process.

The psychological theories of Short-Term and Long-Term memory enter the picture at this point. These two types of memory are hypothesized to explain both the duration and capacity of one's memory. There are volumes of material written on the subject of memory and most of it is based on this dichotomy. One need only look at the latest volume

---

12. James D. Watson, *The Double Helix* (New York: The New American Library, Inc., 1968).

of *The Journal of Verbal Learning and Verbal Behavior* to be brought up to date with current research. Basically the researchers are trying to find out why some information is forgotten very quickly and other information remembered for some extended length of time. Since all of us have taken examinations where we had to recall data collected some time before, we are all familiar with the problems involved with memory. To bring it more into the communication situation, we have all experienced the inability to recall a friend's name while trying to introduce him to another. Now if you can relate that phenomenon to the times you have tried to find the right word to express your thoughts on a particular subject, you can see how important a theory of memory is to the communication theorist.

Much of the information we have accumulated concerning memory comes from our studies involving people who have diseases which cause loss of memory. Most of you have had some acquaintance with the sickness called amnesia. It would appear that this is a disease of recall rather than storage, and is affected either psychologically or physiologically. The forms of amnesia tell us that one may lose his ability to recall information gained through experience, for instance, he cannot remember getting married or going to college, or he may lose his ability to recall impersonal knowledge such as mathematical abilities and abstract concepts. We must assume that this is a problem in recall when after a few months or years either of these types of memory may be regained.[13] Couple with this the disease called aphasia, which is the loss of the ability to use words but does not seem to affect one's ability to conceptualize or experience, and we have the basis for three distinct types of memory: experiential, conceptual, and linguistic.

Discuss these three types of memory in terms of storage and recall.

The three types of memory just mentioned and the two types of storage called Short-Term and Long-Term memory should be considered when one is attempting to formulate a theory of human communication. At this time no one has been able to arrive at a sufficient understanding of these theories to place them in the proper context for the larger theory of communication. The reader is encouraged to develop his own understanding of these theories but at the same time to remember that they are only theories and thus may change drastically over the next few years. The fact that we are gaining more and more information about man and the systems that enable him to communicate means that no theory of human communication can be taken as absolute.

There is still some controversy over how one should define the behavior we have been calling human communication. Perhaps when you reach the conclusion of this book you will realize that there is no

13. J. M. Nielsen, *Memory and Amnesia* (Los Angeles: San Incas Press, 1958).

simple definition for this phenomenon. In recent years the vogue has been to push for totally phenomenological approach to human behavior in which you must consider man as he exists in his total system or environment. This emphasis undoubtedly sprang from the same seed as the area of research known as cybernetics. Cybernetics has to do with feedback and control mechanisms. These mechanisms are always studied in the light of the systems with which they are involved. You should be able to show that systems theory, cybernetics, and the phenomenological approach to human behavior have much in common.

You may be thinking that what has been said in this chapter sounds very complicated, and indeed it is. But one should not underestimate one's mental ability. It should be clear that an individual is almost always aware of himself and what he is saying during a communicative situation. Many times we find that we pay little or no attention to this but our awareness of our behavior is usually high enough to allow us to use the correct grammatical arrangements when we talk, or perform in at least a semiorganized fashion during the involvements of everyday life. A good question to meditate on is, "How did I develop this ability?" The quick answer is, "I learned it." A little reflection on what it means to learn and to implement what you have learned soon makes one realize that there must be something within the individual that controls, directs, or governs his behavior. Actually, one might say that there are many things that perform this task, but the basis of all these things, the system of which they are all a part, we call the human cybernetic.

Psychoanalysts tell us that the human cybernetic begins to develop at about the third month after birth. At this time the baby has sufficient information stored in its brain to be able to begin to evelute incoming sense data. Evaluation precedes decision which precedes behavior. All of these are dependent upon feedback in the form of internal and external signals. Thus, we come to the conclusion that one phase of the human-communication process involves the collection of information by our sense organs; the transformation of this information into neurological impulses; and the transmission of this information to the brain for storage and processing. All this is done with the distinct possibility that the internal signals may be modified from those which would generate the message intended by the communicator. Now we must combine with this the fact that while all of the above is going on, the brain must also monitor its internal and external feedback to keep track of how well it is doing in the present situation.

To give some semblance of structure to these processes and to unite all the systems involved, we have hypothesized a human cybernetic. We shall hear more about this theoretical creature in the next chapter. Suffice it now to say that man, being a self-regulating system, must have some kind of gyro to keep him on course. This is the duty we delegate to the cybernetic. When the system is pushed too fast, this governor slows it down. When it is threatened from the outside, the cybernetic may block the input passages. When we desire to be enlightened, the mind is activated in some way to seek new information. Perhaps it is the cybernetic that performs this function. The human-communication theorist must be aware of the research bearing on the mechanics of the mind.

BIBLIOGRAPHY

1. ALLPORT, FLOYD. *Theories of Perception and the Concept of Structure.* New York: John Wiley, 1955.
2. BERELSON, BERNARD, and STEINER, GARY A. *Human Behavior.* New York: Harcourt, Brace & World, Inc., 1964, pp. 87-132.
3. BROADBENT, D. E. *Perception and Communication.* New York: Pergamon Press, 1958.
4. DELGADO, JOSÉ M. R. *Physical Control of the Mind.* New York: Harper & Row, Publishers, Inc., 1969.
5. DEMBER, WILLIAM N. *The Psychology of Perception.* New York: Henry Holt and Co., 1960.
6. FURLONG, E. J. *A Study in Memory.* London: Thomas Nelson and Sons LTD, 1951.
7. MEREDITH, PATRICK. *Learning Remembering and Knowing.* New York: Association Press, 1961.
8. MERIEAU-PONTY, M. *Phenomenology of Perception,* translated by Colin Smith. New York: The Humanities Press, 1962.
9. MORGAN, CLIFFORD T. *Physiological Psychology.* New York: McGraw-Hill Book Co., 1965.
10. NIELSEN, J. M. *Memory and Amnesia.* Los Angeles: San Lucas Press, 1958.
11. PENFIELD, WILDER, and ROBERTS, LAMAR. *Speech and Brain-Mechanisms.* Princeton: Princeton University Press, 1959.
12. ROSENBLATT, FRANK. *Principles of Neurodynamics.* Washington: Spartan Books, 1962.
13. ROSENBLITH, WALTER A., ed. *Sensory Communication.* Cambridge: The MIT Press, 1961.
14. RUSSELL, W. RITCHIE. *Brain, Memory Learning.* Oxford: The Clarendon Press, 1959.
15. SOLLEY, CHARLES M., and MURPHY, GARDNER. *Development of the Perceptual World.* New York: Basic Books, Inc., 1960.

16. STRAUS, ERWIN. *The Primary World of Senses: A Vindication of Sensory Experience,* translated by Jacob Neadleman. New York: Free Press of Glencoe, 1963.

17. SWETS, JOHN A. *Signal Detection and Recognition by Human Observers.* New York: John Wiley & Sons, Inc., 1964.

18. VON BUDDENBROCK, WOLFGANG. *The Senses.* Ann Arbor: The University of Michigan Press, 1958.

19. ZEIGEN, R. S. *Perceptual Organization: An Investigation of Visual and Auditory Sensory Interaction,* AD 428 258. Washington, D.C.: Office of Technical Service, U.S. Dept. of Commerce, 1964.

Chapter 4

COGNITIVE PROCESSES

At the conclusion of the last chapter we had mentioned a theoretical construct called the cybernetic which we hypothesized as controlling the processing of information by the brain. In this chapter we will point out some of the theories being considered by psychologists to explain our mental activity. In doing this the reader must remember that these theories are the product of man's mind constructing a scheme as to how that mind works. Objective data are very difficult to gather when you do not know what you are looking for. However, the creation of new theories of the mind to account for new data helps to point us in the right direction and leads to a better understanding of our mental processes.

A cybernetic system is one that uses feedback and control mechanisms to regulate its activity within specified limits. The most common example is that of the thermostat in our homes. We set it for a specified temperature, say 72°, and the thermometer in it keeps a continuous check on the temperature of the room. When the temperature drops to a specified lower limit the control mechanism sends a signal to the furnace to start heating the room. When the room temperature is raised to the specified upper limit the thermostat sends another signal to the furnace to shut it off. The important factors in this system are its monitoring ability, its specified upper and lower limits of activity, and its control mechanism.

All living things are to some degree cybernetic systems. Man is the highest form of this type of system we know. The characteristic that makes him tops in this class is his ability to use symbolic functions, that is, he is able to consider phenomenon which are not immediately present. As we shall see in the next chapter this ability to function symbolically is one of his chief forms of control. In this chapter we are interested in seeing how he develops the monitoring system, the control system, and how the limits to his activities are set. In short, we would like to see how his cybernetic system develops and functions.

Although others had posited it before him, Fritz Heider is usually referred to as ushering in the present-day theories on mental balance.[1] The basic assumption of current theories of the mind is that the mind seeks equilibrium—it tends toward homeostasis. Knowing that the mind is dynamic in that it is continually processing information, and that man appears (outwardly) to be static, one must hypothesize that his mental system is a cybernetic system with certain limits within which it can operate. The goal of this system is to maintain the activity of the brain within these limits. If external or internal stimuli cause it to break out of these limits, then we have what society has designated a mentally-ill person. The overload we spoke of in the last chapter is just one way in which this system may be disrupted.

Discuss some of the ways our cybernetic system may be made to malfunction.

If our mind has an innate drive for equilibrium, what are some of the factors involved in this activity? What does the mind strive to keep equal, and what disrupts this equilibrium? How does all of this activity get started in the mind of a baby, and what does this have to do with his later activity. The name of Jean Piaget is firmly entrenched in the research in child development. It is his work that has led us to our major accomplishments in the understanding of the way we acquire knowledge.[2] His work is firmly based on the assumption of equilibrium. He says,

It is thus in terms of equilibrium that we shall try to describe the evolution of the child and the adolescent. From this point of view, mental development is a continuous construction comparable to the erection of a vast building that becomes more solid with each addition. Alternatively, and perhaps more appropriately, it may be likened to the assembly of a subtle mechanism that goes through gradual phases of adjustment in which the individual pieces become more supple and mobile as the equilibrium of the mechanism as a whole becomes more stable. We must, however, introduce an important distinction between two complementary aspects of the process of equilibration. This is the distinction between the variable structures that define the successive states of equilibrium and a certain constant functioning that assures the transition from any one state to the following one.[3]

We have chosen to call this "certain constant functioning that assures the transition from any one state to the following one" the human

1. Fritz Heider, "Attitudes and Cognitive Organization," *Journal of Psychology*, #21 (1946), pp. 107-112.
2. Hans G. Furth, *Piaget and Knowledge* (Englewood Cliffs: Prentice-Hall, Inc., 1969).
3. Jean Piaget, *Six Psychological Studies* (New York: Random House, Inc., A Vintage Book #V-462, 1967), p. 4. Copyright © Random House, Inc.

cybernetic. It is innate and its goal is to maintain equilibrium while the mind passes from one state to another. The states of equilibrium may be looked upon as both quantitative and qualitative levels of knowledge that are time dependent. These levels of knowledge may be viewed as successive planes passing through a cone depicting the accumulation of knowledge to that point in time. Figure 10 is an oversimplified schema depicting only a few of the hundreds of words, concepts, and experiences making up a child's knowledge. As a child develops,

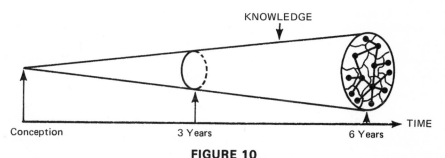

FIGURE 10

A hypothetical schema of the growth of knowledge in terms of the three types of memory: ⌇ = Experiential, ● = Conceptual, / = Linguistic.

he has more experiences, constructs more concepts, and learns more language by which he can tie all of these concepts and experiences together. The interaction of these three types of memory create various ingredients of our personality, such as our desires, fears, emotions, and beliefs. It is the components of these segments of our personality plus the interrelationships among the segments themselves that the cybernetic tries to keep in equilibrium. As new information arrives in our central processing unit, the cybernetic calls upon various subsystems to evaluate and compensate for it. Piaget has developed an elaborate system of schematization, assimilation, and coordination to accomplish this processing. The serious student of human communication should make himself aware of them. (See footnote 2.)

In Figure 10 we can see that the experiential, conceptual, and linguistic memories are intimately related in a very complex network. Even this simple schematic looks complicated, yet it is infinitely less complicated than the real thing. Every concept has several linguistic terms connected with it, as does every experience. On the other hand, every experience probably has more than one concept associated with it, as does every linguistic term. Still, one concept may be associated with many experiences, as may every linguistic term. Osgood's mediation theory is one approach to the understanding of how humans develop meaningful memories.[4] He has developed a scheme of how linguistic terms get attached to various concepts and experiences. His representational model should be understood by the human-communication theorist.

Discuss some of the multiple interactions between experiential, conceptual, and linguistic memories.

As the child develops and his personality takes shape, it is his cybernetic that directs the formulation of the various facets of his personality. One's desires, fears, emotions, and beliefs taken together with the influence of their interrelationships form what Rokeach calls our Attitudinal Frame of Reference.[5] Although one may not be able to verbalize why he does or does not like a certain person or is for or against a certain movement, you can be sure that somewhere in his memory traces there is an entry which effects this feeling. The very core of our evaluative system, that is, the attitudinal frame of reference against which we evaluate all messages, is a system of attitudinal components which are inconceivably intertwined. These desires, fears, emotions, or beliefs are sometimes only vague impressions instilled in us during childhood but nevertheless influencing our cybernetic system.

Many times one can find what the prevailing beliefs of an individual are by analyzing his language. Some concepts seem to predominate at various times in a person's life, such as, the fun life of a young man turns to that of security as he ages. In the same way we manifest our beliefs by the way we fight, vote, or campaign. Some words or slogans take on an almost magical reverence as a result of our belief systems. Un-American, individualism, equality, and the family are examples of concepts that have been or are now strongly-held beliefs. One has only to think back to the McCarthy era or look around him at the civil rights movements to see how beliefs affect human communication.

Most theories of human communication allude to the fact that all incoming messages are filtered through a network of our past experiences to determine what they mean. Further, all outgoing messages are compiled from this same, or a similar, network of experiences. If this is the case, and this seems like a reasonable way of looking at it, then it is clear that these past experiences are of utmost importance to the communication process. Since all incoming data is processed through and all outgoing data is generated from our memories, the stability of our attitudinal frame of reference is of primary importance to our way of life. It is the purpose of our cybernetic to maintain a stable attitudinal frame of reference.

If we believe one thing today and the opposite tomorrow we will probably be very unhappy people. Not knowing what to believe is very

---

4. C. E. Osgood, *Method and Theory in Experimental Psychology* (New York: Oxford University Press, 1953).
5. Milton Rokeach, *The Open and Closed Mind* (New York: Basic Books, Inc., 1960).

distressing. The question is raised though, "How do we know what we believe?" George Miller says, "To say that we believe a proposition implies that, under appropriate circumstances, we would take action or make decisions based on it. In its most general form, therefore, belief is what gives language its powerful control over our behavior. Here again we encounter an unlimited variety of combinations of beliefs that must somehow be related to one another in a systematic fashion. But this is such an ill-formulated topic that I hesitate to pursue it further."[6] We shall not pursue it further either. However, there are other aspects of beliefs that are important to the communication process which we shall pursue.[7]

One way of looking at our beliefs is to consider them as a system. Each individual belief then becomes an element of the system, and the extent to which they are interdependent becomes the relationships. Since this is a cybernetic system it functions under conditions of homeostasis. If this were not true, that is, if when it is disrupted it does not come back to a steady state, then when new information of a contrary nature is introduced into the system, it would disintegrate and we would end up as a babbling idiot. Structural balance among our beliefs must be maintained. How is this accomplished? What theories have we put forth to allow for this type of behavior? One such theory is the open and closed system of Milton Rokeach. He says,

> We assume that, in any situation in which a person must act, there are certain characteristics of the situation that point to the appropriate action to be taken. If the person reacts in terms of such relevant characteristics, his response should be correct, or appropriate. The same situation also contains irrelevant factors, not related to the inner structure or requirements of the situation. To the extent that response depends on such irrelevant factors, it should be unintelligent or inappropriate. Every person, then, must be able to evaluate adequately both the relevant and irrelevant information he receives from every situation. This leads us to suggest a basic characteristic that defines the extent to which a person's system is open or closed; namely, the extent to which the person can receive, evaluate, and act on relevant information received from the outside on its own intrinsic merits, unencumbered by irrelevant factors in the situation arising from within the person or from the outside. Examples of irrelevant internal pressures that interfere with the realistic reception of information are unrelated habits, beliefs, and perceptual cues, irrational ego motives, power needs, the need for self-aggrandizement, the need to allay anxiety, and so forth. By irrelevant external pressures we have in mind most particularly the pressures of reward and punishment arising from external authority; for example, as exerted by parents, peers, other authority figures, reference groups, social and institutional norms, and cultural norms. Will the informa-

6. George Miller, "Language and Psychology," in Eric Lenneberg, ed., *New Directions in the Study of Language* (Cambridge: The M.I.T. Press, 1964), p. 101. Copyright © 1964 by The Massachusetts Institute of Technology.

7. One attempt at understanding the organization and change of belief systems is given by Milton Rokeach in *Beliefs, Attitudes and Values* (San Francisco: Jossey-Bass, Inc., Publishers, 1968).

tion received about a situation from such external sources be evaluated and acted on independently or in accord with expectations about how the external source wishes us to evaluate and act on this information? The more open one's belief system, the more should evaluating and acting on information proceed independently on its own merits, in accord with the inner structural requirements of the situation. Also, the more open the belief system, the more should the person be governed in his actions by internal self-actualizing forces and the less by irrational inner forces. Consequently, the more should he be able to resist pressures exerted by external sources to evaluate and to act in accord with their wishes. One important implication here is that the more open the person's belief system, the more strength should he have to resist externally imposed reinforcements, or rewards and punishments. These should be less effective as determinants of the way information will be evaluated and acted upon.

Conversely, the more closed the belief system, the more difficult should it be to distinguish between information received about the world and information received about the source. What the external source says is true about the world should become all mixed up with what the external source wants us to believe is true, and wants us to do about it. To the extent that a person cannot distinguish the two kinds of information received from the source, he should not be free to receive, evaluate, and act on information in terms of inner requiredness. He should be exposed to pressures, rewards and punishments, meted out by the source designed to make him evaluate and act on the information in the way the source wants him to.[8]

When one is involved in a decision-making situation, he is influenced by at least three variables: (1) the relevant facts; (2) irrelevant facts about the source and the situation; and (3) his own personal needs. These three variables affect his perception of the situation as well as his selection of the important information to be processed. It is much easier to talk about the decision-making situation than it is to behave appropriately when in such a situation. The information one receives is almost always colored by the feelings we have about the informant. If we do not trust him, he could be telling us the truth and we wouldn't accept it. If we do trust him, we never question the validity of the information. How can we know what is truth, especially when our feelings about the source and our personal needs are nearly always stronger than our desire to know the facts? Is it realistic to speak of an open-minded person in Rokeach's terms? Can we in reality separate facts from feelings and desires?

It is certain that there is no truly open-minded person, as there is no truly close-minded person. All of us fit on a continuum somewhere between the two extremes. At the same time it would appear that most of us are closer to the "closed" extreme than to the "open" end. At least that is how we see "others." "They" always seem to pick up irrelevant material upon which to make their decisions. "They" are swept up by the emotions of the situation so that they are incapable of making an

8. Milton Rokeach, *The Open and Closed Mind,* pp. 57, 58.

"objective" decision. But in that "we" feel this way about others, are we not admitting that we let the personality of others influence us too much in our decision-making tasks? This is a very difficult question to answer. May open-mindedness be directly equated with level of education? That is, the more educated a person is the better able he is to be "objective" about his decisions. Think about that.

Discuss the open and closed mind hypothesized by Rokeach and its bearing on our decision-making processes.

The system of Rokeach just mentioned gives us a way of looking at our beliefs without enumerating them. It is a theory well worth the human-communication theorist's time to understand. Its implications are found in many of the other theories set forth by psychologists to explain human behavior. In relation to the mental balance theory, it explains why some people never seem to get upset by information that would seem to be contradictory to their beliefs; they merely discount it as rubbish either because it comes from an unacceptable source or their personal needs are so high they will not accept it as information at all. You may think these people are rather odd, but how many have you known? For them to keep a stable mental structure, they cannot afford to allow disrupting information to enter. Thus, the closed mind functions as a buffer to keep them from the agonies of prolonged indecision. For example, if when you were first confronted with the possibility of taking drugs, you made the decision that drugs were bad and you could not be bothered with them, you might choose to have a closed mind on this subject and just not consider any information about drugs as relevant. This is the easiest way to maintain your equilibrium.

At the same time, we know that the belief system is made up of many components—beliefs that are singular in nature but which we are unable to isolate in practice because of the necessary interaction of other beliefs in the system. These belief-components are kept in structural equilibrium by our cybernetic system. How then can we hold to beliefs that are diametrically opposed, for instance, a member of the SDS votes for Barry Goldwater. We seem to be able to insulate some belief-components from others to such an extent that they never come into confrontation. Thus, we can hold to two opposing beliefs without being "mentally ill" if we can function without them becoming juxtaposed. If, however, a situation arises in which we must bring these two beliefs into our focus on reality at the same time, we are in trouble. Our mind becomes overwrought with the unbalance and we may be in need of professional help. The insulation between two beliefs may be a desire for gain, an emotional dependence, or a fear of reprisal. Thus any segment of our personality may function as an insulator between belief-components. At the same time we may sublimate these two opposing beliefs to such an extent that they cannot be brought into our conscious mind at any single time.

As an example, consider the girl who believes very strongly in the fact that some day a boy will come along and sweep her off her feet; they will be married and live happily ever after. There are many components to this belief, but one of them is the belief that love is the motivating force for boy-girl relationship. Now she meets her knight in shining armor. She is overwhelmed by him. He begins to get "fresh" (on their 20th date). This situation brings up another belief-component that she didn't think would be brought into her conscious mind. Now that it is there, it begins to play havoc with her mental balance. It has always been her belief that premarital sexual relations were wrong. What does she do in a situation like this? She may terminate her relationship with this young man and conclude that he really wasn't her knight in shining armor, thus denying one of her beliefs. She may give in and "go all the way" and so deny another belief. Or she may carry on long and furious discussions on the subject of both belief-components with her lover, herself, and anyone else whom she trusts, and somehow reconcile the three divergent elements in the situation.

A close-minded person would give in to the stronger of the two beliefs immediately and insulate it against the other belief by some other component, such as, fear of being an "old maid" or of "going to hell." The open-minded person would consider the alternatives at some length and then make her decision which, by the way, might be the same as that made by the close-minded person. It should be evident that the open-minded person will have much more conscious mental strain than the close-minded person. Albeit, a well-reasoned decision will probably benefit the individual's mental structure in the long run. There is no experimental evidence for this, however.

As was stated before, most of us are somewhere in the middle of the open and closed mind continuum, and, therefore, would behave in some variation of the above three possibilities. Not knowing the relative strengths of either of the beliefs or their related mental conditions, it is impossible to predict the behavior of any given person in any given situation. In fact, not even that person can make so bold a prediction. The more close-minded we are, the more probable our prediction would be, but we could never be 100% sure.

Discuss the interplay of beliefs, fears, emotions, and desires in explicit situations.

What consequences do the above assumptions have on a theory of human communication? Since we know that all facets of our personality are learned, either through actual experience or abstract knowledge, how can two belief components develop that are logically contradictive? This is indeed a mystery. Yet we know that they do, and that they may never be brought into confrontation. Psychoanalysts tell us that sublimated contradictory beliefs may be the main cause of mental problems.[9] Thus they try to surface these beliefs in hope that they will guide the patient to a meaningful solution to the contradiction. This doesn't always work; the patient sometimes gets worse and ends up in a mental hospital.

We have mentioned that beliefs compose only one facet of our personality. Our general personality is the manifestation of our overall attitudinal frame of reference, which is composed of all our memory systems and their various interactions. We have hypothesized that beliefs are learned and form the underlying structure of our attitudes. Muzafer Sherif says, "When we talk about attitudes, we are talking about what a person has *learned* in the process of becoming a member of a family, a member of a group, and of society that makes him react to his social world in a *consistent* and *characteristic* way, instead of a transitory and haphazard way. We are talking about the fact that he is no longer neutral in sizing up the world around him: he is *attracted* or *repelled, for* or *against, favorable* or *unfavorable.* We are talking about the fact that his behavior toward other persons, groups, institutions, and nations takes on a *consistent* and *characteristic* pattern as he becomes socialized. We are talking about his ties, stands, and sentiments regarding the family and toward various social, religious, political, and economic issues. We are talking about the fact that what we see and listen to are selectively chosen from a mass of potential stimulation surrounding the individual. We refer to how we see ourselves and others after we have attended to some aspect of the multifaceted world about us."[10] The words consistent and characteristic are emphasized in the above quote. These are the two elements of our personality that make it possible for both ourselves and others to know who we are. The degree to which we manifest consistency is the degree to which others identify us as stable individuals. This consistency must exist across many characteristics, however, for we take on many roles in our normal, everyday life. Each time we take on another role we must call upon our cognitive structure to apply itself to this situation.

> The self-identity of the person consists of more than just one commitment or one stand; it is multifaceted. The individual has various identifications, various personal ties, and various personal commitments. Besides being a man or a woman, an individual is a family member with given responsibilities; he represents an occupation with certain pretensions. He is a Republican or Democrat; he is Protestant or Catholic or Jewish. He has abiding stands on various issues; the duties of a father, the standards of performance

9. Sigmund Freud, *Psychopathology of Everyday Life,* trans. A. A. Brill (London: Ernest Benn, Ltd., 1960).

10. Muzafer Sherif, in the introduction to *Attitude, Ego-Involvement, and Change,* edited by Carolyn W. and Muzafer Sherif (New York: John Wiley & Sons, Inc., 1967), p. 2.

in his work, and the responsibilities of citizenship. He has abiding stands on other groups as well as on his own group and on peace and war, civil rights, foreign policy, farm policy, and labor-management issues.[11]

Many of our beliefs, fears, emotions, and desires are role specific, but many of them are more general and transcend the individual roles and manifest their presence in every role we take. Thus we may be a conservative and this characteristic be evident in our political, educational, religious, and social stands. At the same time we find some people who are conservative in their social and religious stands but liberal in their political and educational stands. Each belief is influenced by the situations in which it was learned and the conditions under which it was called into active play—a continuation of our learning experience. Since these experiences are not always consistent, we cannot expect the resulting beliefs to be consistent. And since our cybernetic can only organize what we give it to organize, through our sense organs, it cannot know what is logically consistent unless someone points it out. Thus, we may have logically inconsistent beliefs growing side-by-side until something occurs to point out their inconsistency. If there was such a thing as innate human logicalness, then we would not have to worry about human inconsistencies. But, since there isn't, we must do our best to understand what the basis of various communicators' behavior is.

Discuss the implications of inconsistent behavior in various roles on the communication situation.

We have seen that two or more beliefs (or desires, or fears, or emotions) may be contradictory in nature, and, if this is brought to conscious realization, it causes severe mental strain. Now we would like to go a step further and say that whenever any information is brought to the mind for processing, the processing can take one of two courses. We can assimilate this information into our cognitive structure as reinforcement for an existing mental state, or we can hold it in abeyance for further processing activity because it does not fit into one of our belief structures. Two contradictory beliefs or two pieces of relevant but nonrelatable information are examples of what is called cognitive dissonance. Leon Festinger, the founder of the theory of Cognitive Dissonance, presents the following two hypotheses about this mental condition.

1. The existence of dissonance, being psychologically uncomfortable, will motivate the person to try to reduce the dissonance and achieve consonance.

2. When dissonance is present, in addition to trying to reduce it, the person will actively avoid situations and information which would likely increase the dissonance.

11. Carolyn W. Sherif, Muzafer Sherif, and Roger E. Nebergall, *Attitude and Attitude Change* (Philadelphia: W. B. Saunders Company, 1965), p. 67.

Before proceeding to develop this theory of dissonance and the pressures to reduce it, it would be well to clarify the nature of dissonance, what kind of concept it is, and where the theory concerning it will lead. The two hypotheses stated above provide a good starting point for this clarification. While they refer here specifically to dissonance, they are in fact very general hypotheses. In place of "dissonance" one can substitute other notions similar in nature, such as "hunger," "frustration," or "disequilibrium," and the hypotheses would still make perfectly good sense.

In short, I am proposing that dissonance, that is, the existence of nonfitting relations among cognitions, is a motivating factor in its own right. By the term *cognition,* I mean any knowledge, opinion, or belief about the environment, about oneself, or about one's behavior. Cognitive dissonance can be seen as an antecedent condition which leads to activity oriented toward dissonance reduction just as hunger leads to activity oriented toward hunger reduction.[12]

When information comes into our central processor and it is found to be dissonant with the information in our cognitive structure, we must do something with it. We have just said that the mind holds it in abeyance until it can determine what should be done with it. This period of review is different for each individual. In the example of the female's belief system used earlier, we hypothesized that the close-minded individual would resolve this dissonance quickly by isolating one of the two conflicting beliefs. The open-minded person would take longer to review the situation and bring more information to bear on the problem. We should hasten to add that there is a crucial period of time when one slips from open-mindedness to mental weakness. Both personalities go through a period of instability in which one would hope that more information would precipitate a decision on the matter. The difference between the two personalities is that the former comes to a decision while the latter continues to oscillate from one position to the other.

What the mind does with incoming information is determined by the amount of discrepancy between it and the information already stored in the mind in the form of beliefs. Confirmatory information (consonant) will reinforce presently-held beliefs, while contradictory information (dissonant) must be accounted for by the cybernetic in such a way that it does not disrupt the equilibrium of our cognitive structure. As we have seen some times this is accomplished by rationalizing our position, discounting the source, or insulating our beliefs by closing them. However, since the mind is continuously active, it may be working on the conciliation of two divergent beliefs in its subconsciousness even while we are worrying about something else. This conciliatory action may be the stimulus for many of our dreams. In view of what we have said about the open and closed mind, which would likely have the

---

12. Leon Festinger, "An Introduction to the Theory of Dissonance," in E. P. Hollander and Raymond G. Hunt (eds.), *Current Perspectives in Social Psychology* (New York: Oxford University Press, 1963), p. 352.

most active dream production? How do you conciliate your divergent beliefs? Or how do you decrease the dissonance level when you come in contact with information that is contradictory to one of your beliefs?

Discuss the various means you can think of for dissonance reduction.

How much dissonance can you stand? If you look at your thought processes you will probably see that you have built up a cognitive buffer to insulate you from much of the dissonance producing information that you could receive. Referring back to the quote from Festinger we see that he hypothesized that we would naturally avoid situations that might present dissonance producing information. If you don't receive it you don't have to process it. Thus, we may exercise some choice in our information gathering behavior. This in turn affects our overall communicative behavior. What we are saying is that most of us tend to become more like we are; we seek reinforcing information and shy away from dissonance producing information. We do this to maintain some semblance of mental balance and keep our information processing activity to a minimum. In most cases we would not diagnose this as passivity; rather it is a means of survival. Information overload was discussed in Chapter 3. The more disequilibrium existing in our mental structure the more mental activity we must have to decrease the dissonance. This produces the same effect as information overload.

We have now seen that theoretically there are at least two motivating forces in our cognitive structure, that is, dissonance and our attitudinal frame of reference. Our attitudinal frame of reference motivates us to seek positive reinforcement and thus cause our lives to continue along a straight line. Cognitive dissonance is a motivating force that pushes us back to the straight line after we have received some information that has jarred us from our course. Both of these theories are based on the underlying assumption that the mind tends toward equilibrium among its parts: a cybernetic system. Both theories are extremely important to the human-communication theorist if he expects to understand how man sees himself.

We have looked at how the cognitive structure behaves toward dissonant information and/or beliefs. Now let us look at some of the theories of how a belief may be changed. If we believe that population control is wrong and have catalogued a number of arguments against it, how can this belief be changed to the opposite? Is it possible to take a person who does not believe in population control and turn him into an active worker for population control? What would it take to do this? Answers to these questions have been put forth continuously since man has been able to communicate. Much of our communication is concerned with varying degrees of the persuasion process. Outstanding examples of the fact that this can be done are Hitler's marshalling the German people behind him in the thirties and the Christian evangelistic crusades of the past 19 centuries. Thus we see it can happen.

If you remember the example on premarital sex you will recall that it was hypothesized that a confrontation such as that would make the person change one of her beliefs. But supposing you do not have two logically contradictory beliefs? Festinger says that cognitive dissonance is a motivating force for changing beliefs. You probably will agree with that. Thus, it would seem that all we have to do is bring about a state of cognitive dissonance. But how do you know when cognitive dissonance occurs in the mind of the communicatee? The feedback you get may help, but this is often purposefully misleading. It would seem then that you can use this feedback only as a tentative indication of the receiver's mental state, and rather than relying on it entirely (in most situations) you should have a plan in mind as to how you will proceed to lead your audience to the desired goal. The information referred to in Chapter 2 (page 28) should be reviewed at this time as it is germane to this discussion. Going along with this theory is that of Sherif, Sherif, and Nebergall. They state, "Stripped to its bare essential, the problem of attitude change is the problem of the degree of discrepancy from communication and the felt necessity of coping with the discrepancy. The discrepancy in question is the degree of divergence between the position advocated in a communication or message and the own position of the subject exposed to it. Of course, psychologically, the discrepancy in question is the divergence experienced or felt by the individual between the position he upholds and the position to which he is exposed."[13]

We have been looking at attitudes as being the outward manifestation of a belief system. Thus if we can change an attitude we might surmise that we are changing the belief that underlies it. The controversy over whether any of our experimental evidence proves that an attitude has been changed still exists. It usually takes the form of long-term vs short-term change. If you change a person's verbal response to an opinion questionnaire, have you really changed his attitude, his behavior, or his belief? Much more evidence is needed before any kind of an answer can be given to this question. The felt need of the recipient of a communiqué will certainly have an effect on how he responds to it, but will the mental activity generated by it cause a lasting effect in his belief system? Even if the discrepancy is too large for the receiver to assimilate into his cognitive structure, it will have some effect on this structure. It is hard to believe that any mental activity can go unnoticed by the brain.

The emphasis on the amount of discrepancy between the attitudes of the receiver and the point of the communiqué points us back to what has been said about the acceptance and rejection of information by our cybernetic system. If the discrepancy is too great we will reject it with hardly more thought. However, if it is within the range of believability,

---

13. In *Attitude and Attitude Change*, p. 225.

we will have to spend more time on it. It has been theorized that each individual has formed latitudes of acceptance and rejection of information on those subjects with which they are involved. There are other subjects with which they choose to remain noncommitted; this does not mean that they remain uninvolved. Sherif and Sherif define these concepts as follows:

1. *Latitude of acceptance:* That segment that includes the own position of the person on the issue, plus other positions he will tolerate around his own position.

2. *Latitude of rejection:* That segment that includes the position on the issue most objectionable (obnoxious) to the person, plus other positions also objectionable to him.

3. *Latitude of noncommitment:* That range on which the individual expresses neither acceptance nor rejection—for reasons of his own.[14]

Latitudes of acceptance, rejection, and noncommitment are based on the assumption that individuals have taken a position on the subject at hand. This position, or attitude, is the manifestation of a deeper cognitive structure we have called a belief system. Our attitudes reflect our commitments to a system of beliefs. We say system of beliefs because it is nearly impossible to isolate a single belief and say that it is the influencing agent for any given attitude. Attitudes are only visible when a person is put into a situation where his commitment to a portion of his belief system is relevant. Our commitment then becomes a stimulus for our resultant behavior. Thus, attitudes are manifest in behaviors which reflect the commitment we have to a system of beliefs. The latitudes of acceptance, rejection, and noncommitment are the distances from the positions we are willing to consider as relevant. According to Sherif and Sherif we have established norms within our cognitive structure around which we evaluate incoming information to see if we will tolerate it. If we cannot, we will reject it or let it lie dormant in our pool of noncommitment.

What does this say about the process of opinion change? Referring back to Footnote 13 we see that one must determine what the latitudes of acceptance, rejection, and noncommitment of his audience are so that he can strive to present information that will fall somewhere within their latitude of acceptance and thus be considered. In other words, a communicator trying to persuade should have a pretty good idea of the belief structure of his audience and their toleration limits. If his arguments fall outside these toleration limits, they will be ineffective; either because they will be rejected or fall into their area of noncommitment. This sounds like an impossible task. However, it appears that social norms will define a latitude of acceptance and rejection.[15] Therefore,

14. Muzafer Sherif and Carolyn W. Sherif, *Social Psychology* (New York: Harper & Row, Publishers, 1969), p. 296.

15. Sherif and Sherif, *Social Psychology,* p. 192.

one who knows his subject well and knows something about the normal behavior of human beings in connection with his subject should be able to guess fairly accurately about how far he can go in each argument he presents. If he can, then he may construct his arguments in such a way as to lead the audience gently to the goal of his persuasive discourse.

We have mentioned the concepts of commitment and noncommitment several times and perhaps we should explain these concepts a little more at this point. Given a particular subject each one of us has various beliefs about it to which we have varying degrees of commitment. Take the subject of religion. We may be absolutely committed to the belief in a god. When someone talks to us about this subject we are willing to discuss various concepts of what God might be and even delve into the philosophical and psychological necessities for the existence of God. These concepts all fall within our latitude of acceptance. The argument that the concept God is a figment of our imagination is completely objectionable to us, and discussions of how this concept arose out of societal needs and human weaknesses fall into our latitude of rejection. However, we remain noncommitted on the argument that one god is better than another so that arguments on the relative worth of the Christian, Buddhist, Taoist, or Hindu God fall into our latitude of noncommitment.

As you can see, the above positions pretty well define our commitments to a belief in God. The concept of commitment may be equated with Sherif and Sherif's concept of ego-involvement.[16]

> Operationally, the degree of a person's ego-involvement in ongoing psychological activity is inferred from the relative magnitudes of his latitudes of acceptance, rejection, and noncommitment in categorizing the relevant stimulus domain: The greater the size of the latitude of rejection relative to the latitude of acceptance and the latitude of noncommitment, the greater is the person's ego-involvement in that stimulus domain.

This is to say that the narrower one's latitude of acceptance of information dissonant to his position on a given subject, the more committed he is to that position. All other information is relegated to the large bins of rejection and noncommitment. This behavior also smacks of what we spoke of earlier in this chapter when talking about open and close-mindedness: the closed mind being one which will not consider information that is very dissonant with the position to which it is committed. High commitment or ego-involvement necessitate closing this belief to most of the dissonant information relevant to this belief. The reason for this would appear to be that the extreme amount of information processing it would take to assimilate this dissonant information into one's belief system would overload the central nervous system, for instance, assimilation of this dissonant information might necessitate a

16. *Social Psychology,* p. 388.

complete restructuring of one's belief system in a relatively short time. This would be traumatic.

Discuss the relationships between the concepts open and closed mind and that of ego-involvement.

It is hoped that the reader realizes that the theories on the activities of the mind are all highly speculative but are presented here because they seem to explain man's cognitive behavior best within the present state of our knowledge. The question that we are now considering, to wit: How is one's opinion changed? is a crucial issue in any theory of human communication. Surely we realize that learning changes our opinions and that a state of cognitive dissonance is certainly conducive to a change of opinion. We have mentioned several variables that are hypothesized to be active in the process of opinion change. All of these variables are based on the assumption that the mind strives toward equilibrium. Before going further perhaps we should say a word about opinions.

There is general confusion about the similarities and differences among opinions, attitudes, and beliefs. Some writers use all three synonymously while others will use only one pair this way, and still others insist that all three have distinct meanings. The most popular definition seems to be that opinions are verbalized attitudes, and attitudes are feelings derived from subconscious beliefs. (Under this definition all beliefs are subconscious.) Although there seems to be a general progression from subconscious to verbalized, it is impossible to arrive at a general definition for these terms. Therefore, the reader must always be aware of the ambiguity surrounding them whenever they are used.

Another thought that should be kept in mind is that one must be concerned with both the direction of the attitude (favorable-unfavorable) and the commitment to this attitude. The first is relatively simple to ascertain. The second is much more difficult—as we have seen. However, in light of mental balance and dissonance theory, the second is the more important of the two. How dissonant can a message be from a stated belief before it exceeds the latitude of acceptance that this individual has? The strength of our commitment is directly related to this latitude of acceptance, and this to the possibility of opinion change. There are other factors that enter in, but one must certainly concern himself with this factor when investigating the effect of a communiqué.

What other factors should be considered when investigating the process of opinion change? A Little thought will let you come up with many. One that was proposed many centuries ago by Aristotle and continues to be confirmed by present-day experiments is the influence of the speaker (communicator).[17] The listener's attitude toward the speaker has a stronger influence on resultant opinion change than any

17. George A. Borden, "A Quantitative Study of Reactions of the Open and Closed Mind to Persuasive Discourse," Unpublished Ph.D. Thesis, Cornell University, 1964.

other variable. Under the assumptions of mental balance we can write an equation using operationally defined variables and predict in what direction and to what extent opinion will be changed. Osgood, Suci, and Tannenbaum did this using only three variables: attitude toward the speaker, toward the content of the communiqué, and the position the speaker takes on the topic.[18]   Thus if I have a high regard for the speaker, I am strongly in favor of population control, and he speaks against population control, my opinion toward population control will become less favorable. At the same time, my opinion of the speaker will decrease, thus, maintaining my mental balance. This is referred to as the "Congruity Principle." The interaction of interdependent variables will precipitate a change in attitude in the direction of the resultant force.

Other researchers have added more variables to the equation for attitude change, including those of ego-involvement and latitudes of acceptance, rejection, and noncommitment. The results indicate that we have a long way to go before we understand the cognitive processes sufficiently to put all the pieces together. However, we are making progress, and this is a very important area for the human-communication theorist to work. Perhaps a brief summary will help to crystallize these concepts.

Summary:

It is only a short intellectual step from the idea that man's mind is composed of an intertwined set of beliefs to the concept of mental balance. Theories based on this concept hypothesize that the brain's natural goal is to maintain equilibrium among the several belief systems. Though this is a rather mechanistic way of looking at human mental activities, it seems to be the clearest way to get the reader to understand something about how the mind functions. If you will remember that all theories are idealistic in nature and, therefore, only suggestive of reality, you will be able to gain some insights into how man thinks the human mental processes function.

If one accepts the concept of mental balance as basic to mental activities, he can then imagine how these processes function. When information is fed into the brain through the senses it is evaluated in light of the belief systems residing there. The new information may have nothing to do with some of the belief systems while it may reinforce others and contradict still others. The first type of information we neglect, the second we accept readily, but the third we must consciously examine and justify our disposition of it. It is this third type of information that interests us most.

18. Charles E. Osgood, George J. Suci, and Percy H. Tannenbaum, *The Measurement of Meaning* (Urbana: University of Illinois Press, 1957), p. 200.

Seldom do we take part in communication acts where all the information we receive is either inconsequential or reinforcing to existing beliefs. Usually there is some information which causes us to think. Much of this cogitation may take place subconsciously. As a result of the reception of this information our mental balance is disrupted until we can rationalize the existence of this information. We call the condition of the mind that is caused by this temporary disruption cognitive dissonance. Of course, some people can live with more dissonance than others. Thus, we see some people disregarding information that makes us terribly upset. Since the mind is a rather mysterious organ, we are not sure exactly why one person is affected while another is not.

The theory of cognitive dissonance is built upon the premise that after one makes a decision he must evaluate succeeding information in such a way that it fits into his prescribed format. The verification of the theory was accomplished by using sharply discrete well-defined decisions. However, a more realistic way of looking at man's mental processes is to visualize a continuous stream of minor decisions with now and then a major one. If this is our model then we see that our latitude of acceptance, rejection, and noncommitment will produce varying degrees of debate of incoming information. This means that any one of the many decisions may set up a dissonance situation. A theory of persuasion should be obvious.[19] The main difficulty is that we can seldom be sure when a dissonance situation exists in another person's mind.

BIBLIOGRAPHY

1. ADORNO, T. W.; FRENKEL-BRUNSWICK, ELSE; LEVINSON, DANIEL; and SANFORD, R. NEVITT. *The Authoritarian Personality.* New York: Harper & Row, 1950.

2. ANDERSON, RICHARD, and AUSUBEL, DAVID. *Readings in the Psychology of Cognition.* New York: Holt, Rinehart & Winston, Inc., 1965.

3. BINDRA, DALBIR. *Motivation.* New York: The Ronald Press Company, 1959.

4. BRUNER, JEROME; GOODNOW, JACQUELINE; and AUSTON, GEORGE. *A Study of Thinking.* New York: John Wiley & Sons, Inc., 1956.

5. BREHM, JACK, and COHEN, ARTHUR. *Explorations in Cognitive Dissonance.* New York: John Wiley & Sons, 1962.

6. BROWN, ROGER. *Social Psychology.* New York: The Free Press, 1965.

19. George A. Borden, "Cognitive Dissonance: A Theory of Persuasion," *The Pennsylvania Speech Annual,* 1965, pp. 43-50.

7. FESTINGER, LEON. *A Theory of Cognitive Dissonance.* Evanston, Ill.: Row-Peterson, 1957.

8. ———. *Conflict, Decision and Dissonance.* Stanford: Stanford University Press, 1964.

9. FREUD, SIGMUND. *Psychopathology of Everyday Life.* Trans. A. A. Brill. London: Ernest Benn, Ltd., 1960.

10. FURTH, HANS G. *Piaget And Knowledge.* Englewood Cliffs: Prentice-Hall, Inc., 1969.

11. GAGNÉ, ROBERT. *The Conditions of Learning.* New York: Holt, Rinehart & Winston, Inc., 1965.

12. HARPER, ROBERT; ANDERSON, CHARLES; CHRISTENSEN, CLIFFORD; and HUNKA, STEVEN, (eds.). *The Cognitive Processes: Readings.* Englewood Cliffs: Prentice-Hall, Inc., 1964.

13. HEBB, D. O. *The Organization of Behavior.* New York: John Wiley & Sons, 1949.

14. HOLLANDER, E. P., and HUNT, RAYMOND. *Current Perspectives in Social Psychology.* New York: Oxford University Press, 1963.

15. HUNT, EARL B. *Concept Learning: An Information Processing Problem.* New York: John Wiley & Sons, 1962.

16. HUNT, J. McV. *Intelligence and Experience.* New York: The Ronald Press Co., 1961.

17. KNAPP, PETER. *Expression of the Emotions in Man.* New York: International Universities Press, Inc., 1963.

18. LENNEBERG, ERIC. *New Directions in the Study of Language.* Cambridge: The M.I.T. Press, 1964.

19. MILLER, GEORGE; GALANTER, EUGENE; and PRIBRAM, KARL. *Plans and the Structure of Behavior.* New York: Holt, Rinehart & Winston, Inc., 1960.

20. NEWCOMB, THEODORE; TURNER, RALPH; and CONVERSE, PHILIP. *Social Psychology.* New York: Holt, Rinehart & Winston, Inc., 1965.

21. OSGOOD, CHARLES. *Method and Theory in Experimental Psychology.* New York: Oxford University Press, 1953.

22. ———, SUCI, G., and TANNENBAUM, P. *The Measurement of Meaning.* Urbana: The University of Illinois Press, 1957.

23. ——— and SEBEOK, THOMAS, (eds.). *Psycholinguistics: A Survey of Theory and Research Problems.* Bloomington, Ind.: Indiana University Press, 1965.

24. PIAGET, JEAN. *Play, Dreams and Imitation in Childhood.* Trans. G. Gattegne and F. M. Hodgson. New York: W. W. Norton & Company, Inc., 1962.

25. ———. *Psychology of Intelligence.* Trans. Malcolm Piercy and D. E. Berlyne. Totowa, N.J.: Littlefield, Adams & Co., 1969.

26. ———. *Six Psychological Studies.* Trans. Anita Tenzer. New York: Random House, Inc., 1967.

27. ———. *The Construction of Reality in the Child.* Trans. Margaret Cook. New York: Basic Books, 1954.

28. REITMAN, WALTER R. *Cognition and Thought.* New York: John Wiley & Sons, Inc., 1965.

29. ROKEACH, MILTON. *Beliefs, Attitudes and Values.* San Francisco: Jossey-Bass, Inc., Publishers, 1968.

30. ———. *The Open and Closed Mind.* New York: Basic Books, Inc., 1960.

31. SHERIF, MUZAFER, and SHERIF, CAROLYN W. *Social Psychology.* New York: Harper & Row, Publishers, 1969.

32. ——— (eds.). *Attitude, Ego-Involvement, and Change.* New York: John Wiley & Sons, Inc., 1967.

33. SHERIF, CAROLYN; SHERIF, MUZAFER; and NEBERGALL, ROGER. *Attitude and Attitude Change.* Philadelphia: W. B. Saunders Co., 1965.

34. STEINER, IVAN, and FISHBEIN, MARTIN. *Current Studies in Social Psychology.* New York: Holt, Rinehart & Winston, Inc., 1965.

35. THOMSON, ROBERT. *The Psychology of Thinking.* Baltimore: Pelican Books, 1959.

36. WEINBERG, HARRY L. *Levels of Knowing and Existence.* New York: Harper & Brothers, 1959.

Chapter 5

HUMAN
COMMUNICATIVE
BEHAVIOR

In the last two chapters we have been talking about the processes involved in receiving and processing information. The recipient of a signal has many built-in obstacles to effective communication. We have mentioned some of these, and you have probably thought of many more. We observed that the human processing of information involves many processes of which we have very little knowledge, and which cannot be recognized firsthand to gain more knowledge. We are able to develop theories about these processes only because we can observe the behavior of the recipient of a signal. Thus, these theories are inferences based on observable behavior, but behavior that is somewhat removed from the point of processing. This makes theories of cognitive functions very tenuous, however brilliant they may be.

What may be learned by observing the behavior of a human reacting to a signal transmitted by another human or some other entity in his environment? It has been demonstrated that when the internal systems of a human are stimulated they react in a generally predictable manner. At one time it was felt that this reaction was consistent enough to be studied in what came to be known as stimulus-response psychology.[1] It has since been shown that stimulus-response theory, though adequate to explain some behaviors, is not adequate to explain verbal behavior.[2] Though verbal behavior is only one of the many ways man communicates, it has come to be considered the primary means of communication. We shall consider this assumption later in this chapter. Now we would like to try to ascertain just what communicative behavior is.

1. B. F. Skinner, *Verbal Behavior* (New York: Appleton-Century-Crofts, 1957).
2. Noam Chomsky, "A Review of B. F. Skinner's VERBAL BEHAVIOR," in Jerry A. Fodor and Jerrold J. Katz (eds.), *The Structure of Language* (Englewood Cliffs: Prentice-Hall, Inc., 1964).

As you know, psychology is the science of human behavior. Psychologists are interested in how a person reacts to a stimulus. In this way they try to determine how humans act in given situations, primarily so that they may generate a theory of the mind from this observed behavior. In this sense we may say that psychology is primarily interested in general human behavior and the theories of the mind that would predict this behavior. How does communicative human behavior differ from general human behavior? The answer is, it doesn't. The behavior may very well be identical, in fact, the same behavior may be classified as general human behavior by one psychologist and communicative human behavior by another; the difference being only in the mind of the observer. At the same time it may be impossible to determine which observer is right when looking at the situation from the position of the behavior source. It would appear, then, that there may be at least two ways of defining communicative human behavior; for example, from the point of view of the sender of the signal and from the point of view of the receiver of the signal.

From the point of view of the receiver of a signal, any human behavior becomes communicative when it generates a message in his mind. To do this the receiver must assume that the behavior is symbolic; that is, it represents some desire of the sender other than the desire to partake in that behavior. A symbol stands for or represents something other than itself. Therefore, symbolic behavior is behavior that is meant to evoke a message in a receiver other than "that is the way he behaves." We attach some other meaning to the behavior; such as, he is behaving that way because he wants. . . . We feel that he is behaving that way because it will evoke a message other than recognition that the act was performed. We are often so well tuned into this channel of communication, that is, we assume every act is intended to communicate, that we say, "It is *obvious* that he meant to . . . ," when it isn't the obvious message at all. We can describe general human behavior by saying he did this, this, this and this; when we attach meaning to it (or decode meaning from it), that is, we assume a communicative intent, we turn it into communicative behavior.

There are several different levels at which this transformation may occur. For example, a girl wears a very short mini-skirt to class. As general behavior, it is normal for people to wear clothes. Since it is a warm day, the less clothing the better. She is reacting to her environment and trying to keep cool. If you are asked to look at this behavior as communicative behavior, you might say that she is trying to tell the people she comes in contact with that she is in the now generation and wants to wear the styles of the day. A very conservative religious person might think she is saying, "I'm on the make." A less conservative person might think she is communicating her vain, ego-centered pride. You may be able to think of many other messages this type of behavior might evoke. The real question is, what is she trying to communicate? The answer may be, nothing. This may just be her general behavior, and there may be no ulterior meaning there. One characteristic of people is that we are unwilling to take general human behavior as simply that. We are always looking for the hidden meaning. Thus, we can say that all human behavior may be communicative behavior if we translate it as such. However, the message may only be in the mind of the receiver.

Discuss the possibility that subconsciously there is always a message in every signal we transmit because a receiver can always generate one from it.

Now, what about communicative behavior from the point of view of the source of this behavior? When is your behavior communicative? Most of us would say, when it is intended to be communicative. Here again we have a source of ambiguity. Do you always know what or when you intend to communicate? Surely intention lies on a continuum from "no conscious desire" to "total dedication" to communicate. When we are conscious of our desire to communicate, we usually consider the receiver of our signals and try to adapt them to him. In other words, we look at the message in our mind and try to figure the probability of evoking that message in the mind of our receiver given the various types of signals we might transmit. Then we transmit the signals with the highest probability of success. The most obvious cases are those of the advertiser and politician shown in Chapter 3. There are times when we know we are trying to communicate, and when we know that communication has occurred. However, in either case it is nearly impossible to tell whether the message our signals generated in the mind of the receiver is really the one we intended.

Another way of looking at the difference between general human behavior and communicative behavior is to consider the American definitions of sign and symbol. We defined sign as any observable signal that is an integral part of a happening. No message is attached to it. Thus, talking is a sign that a person is alive; the absence of this sign may have many meanings. A symbol is something that stands for something else. Thus talking may be a symbol of aggressiveness, or fear, or joy, etc. Sign behavior is general behavior; symbolic behavior is communicative behavior. Communication can only be present when symbols are present. These symbols may exist only in the mind of the sender or the receiver, in which case faulty communication occurs. If the symbols exist in both the mind of the sender and the receiver, there is less likelihood of faulty communication but still a good chance for it.

In this chapter we are primarily interested in the symbols used by a communicator to transmit a signal which will be received and decoded by a communicatee. If he has encoded a message and transmitted the resulting signal, he has a right to hope that the receiver will understand the message after he has decoded it from the signals received. Yet there is no guarantee of this. The code we use has much to do with the resultant message decoded by the receiver. If the sender is very proficient in encoding messages, he may, after considerable analysis of his receiver, be able to encode a message that the receiver will have no difficulty in decoding at all. At the same time he may be able to encode a message that appears to be the exact opposite of what it really is, and the receiver gets the wrong message from the code he received. We have all been in situations where we were not sure of the sender's intention, knowing that we could decode several messages from the signals he had sent us. We usually end up in this predicament when two or more signals being transmitted contradict each other, but this may well occur within a single signal medium.

Discuss sources of misunderstanding in both single and multiple signal communiqués.

Since we have defined signal as coded meaning, the ability of the encoder and the decoder is a variable that must be taken into account when considering the sources of ambiguity. There is no signal that cannot be interpreted in more than one way, that is, there is no unambiguous signal. Given any signal in any situation, with a little effort you will find that you can decode two or more meanings from it. Our communicative behavior is based on this fact in that we have built into every signal a tremendous amount of redundancy. The redundancy in the English language is said to be fifty per cent or more, depending upon what level one wants to measure this variable, namely, phonemic, morphemic, lexemic, or intermedia. If this is true, then we know that we always have at least twice as much information as we need to decode any particular message. A little thought will let you see that this also is a source of ambiguity. The more signals one has to decode, the more chance there is that he may decode the wrong message from one of them, and, since the overall message is the result of the total decoding process and each successive decoding phase is dependent upon the preceding one, we can easily be led astray by our own decoding processes.

What does this say about the communication process? Whereas we tend to think of this process as a focusing process, it may be a blurring process. It should be the intention of the communicator to make all of the signals he is transmitting force the receiver toward a single message. Thus, all our signals during a communication event should be complimentary. However, it usually happens that some extraneous signals are transmitted and the resultant message may be blurred by them. The amount of blurring is dependent upon both the number and force of the extraneous signals and the selective perception of the receiver. He may not be able to sort out the primary from the extraneous signals.

At the same time the possibility exists that he may focus on one of the extraneous signals as the primary source of the message and thus miss the whole meaning of the communicative act.

We cannot say enough about the possibility of ambiguity in the communication process. Many of our confrontation situations, both at home and abroad, are the result of ambiguities in the communication process. Even with the amount of redundancy built into an ordinary communication situation we are often unable to determine exactly what was the intent of the communicator. This is not to say that if we really knew what his intent was we would always agree with him, but certainly we would have a better chance if we knew absolutely what was his intent. Is he merely expressing his frustration or does he have a legitimate point for us to consider? If he is expressing his frustration, should we not look for the source of the frustration rather than the apparent intended message of his communicative act? How can we get behind the camouflage of the signal to the real intent of the communicator? To do this we must find out who the communicator is in terms of his roles within his identification group and the image that has been created in our minds of this person.[3]

Discuss the concepts of intent, redundancy, and ambiguity in the human-communication process.

By now you should be thinking about the importance of the signals transmitted by a communicator in any given communication situation. A sloppy communicator (in terms of the signals he transmits) cannot expect to be understood by his audience, whether it consists of one or a thousand people. We see abundant evidence of this during every election campaign, whether on the local or national level. Student movements, demonstrations, protests, and the like provide other examples of this phenomenon. The ambiguity surrounding most of these communication situations makes us ask ourselves if the communicators themselves know what their intent is. The signals become so confused that it is nearly impossible to sort out the meaningful from the extraneous.

Communication occurs when our cognitive processes are activated either by a thought brought into our consciousness as a result of an external stimulus or by an internal stimulus that provokes us to action. When either of these events occurs we must make a decision as to what communicative behavior is appropriate for the situation. Having decided this we then encode the message we desire and transmit the resulting signals. Our cognitive decisions are usually made subconsciously, that is, we are not aware of the decision-making process either

---

3. See parts two and three of Borden, Gregg, and Grove, *Speech Behavior and Human Interaction,* for an analysis of what the individual brings to a communication situation ulterior to the immediate transmitted signals.

to respond, what type of response, or the makeup of the signals to be transmitted. We very seldom, if ever, distinguish between the two types of codes available to us for these signals, namely, verbal and nonverbal. We are probably more aware of the verbal code, however. Since the verbal code may be transmitted either vocally (speech) or nonvocally (written), we are usually quite conscious of the decision as to which one we will use if the situation would allow either mode.

We will not attempt to draw a clear distinction between verbal and nonverbal communicative behavior. Suffice it to say that a verbal signal consists of words and their syntactic relations while nonverbal signals consist of all other overt actions from which we may generate a message. Writing is clearly verbal; our appearance and bodily action are clearly nonverbal. But what about the inflection, rate and pitch of our voice when we speak? Into which category would you put them? It doesn't really matter, but it does help one to see the multiplicity of the signals transmitted during any given communication event if we attempt to categorize each subsignal as verbal or nonverbal. You will probably find that you are so proficient at communicating that you cannot even determine all of the signals being sent during any given communication event. This makes it very difficult to study the communication process.

Discuss several specific communication events and delineate the various signals being transmitted ranking them in decreasing order of importance.

Why is it that we are unaware of the many signals we transmit during the communication process? How have we developed the ability to communicate at all? Speculation runs wild on this question. Twentieth-century American psychologists, dominated by the behaviorist's point of view, have leaned heavily on the stimulus-response model of behavior. Their theories have talked about reinforcement and deprivation in terms of the stimulus and the resulting response (behavior).[4] Reinforcement of desired responses to given stimuli are supposed to aid in the learning of these responses and in this way cultivate the "correct" communicative behavior (either verbal or nonverbal) in the child. This theory sounds good until one gets into the very complex behaviors involved in verbal communication. Since we do not learn a single response to a given stimulus, indeed, since any verbal stimulus is almost certain to be unique, in that it will never be repeated, it would be impossible to learn the appropriate responses to given stimuli. A little reflection reveals that this is true in the nonverbal codes as well. How then do we learn to encode appropriate responses to any communicative event?

We mentioned Jean Piaget in connection with cognitive development in Chapter 4. Now we must return to his work in connection with

---

4. Skinner, *Verbal Behavior.*

the development of communicative behavior.[5] Piaget would have us look at language acquisition or the development of communicative behavior in terms of the entire human developmental process. Thus, one cannot study just language acquisition without considering the other aspects of the child's development at the same time. As a child passes from birth to about age 12 he develops an ability to communicate which far exceeds that of any other animal. Part of this is due to his acquisition of language but a greater part is due to his ability to participate in symbolic behavior in general. Though most of us have grown up with the idea that verbal behavior is our primary or perhaps our only form of symbolic behavior, we should take note of the fact that this is not true. It is hoped that the remainder of this chapter will indicate why.

There appears to be three prerequisites to language acquisition: appropriate sensory acuity, symbolic functioning, and pattern recognition.[6] We have already discussed some of the requirements of the sense organs (Chapter 3), and it should be apparent that unless a child has some form of input the brain will not mature, since maturation only proceeds with stimulation. The degree to which a child has normal input channels, primarily auditory, visual, and tactile, will influence his development of appropriate communicative behavior. Deficiencies may just slow up this developmental process or it may stop it altogether. Since there seems to be a critical age at which certain neurological functions must develop it is important that a sensory deficiency be diagnosed as early in a child's life as possible. Our technological advancements may then be able to help the child develop normally.

In the very early stages of development a child exhibits habitual behavior much like that of any other animal and can be subjected to many of the learning processes indigenous to stimulus-response psychology with predictable results. (Hold a young, breast-fed infant in the appropriate position and watch him turn his head and open his mouth expecting to be fed.) He learns to discriminate between stimuli, to abstract necessary information from stimuli, and to generalize about these stimuli from the information available. However, what he is doing in the process is not just learning an appropriate response for a given stimulus, but rather developing schemes which will allow him to generalize about thousands of stimuli to which he has not yet been subjected. These schemes become part of his cognitive structure and he reacts to an input stimulus in light of its interaction with his cognitive structure. He first learns to coordinate the senses in perception. The eye-hand

5. For specific details of Piaget's theories see his books *Six Psychological Studies* (A Vintage Book, V-462), 1967, and *Play, Dreams and Imitation in Childhood* (The Norton Library, N171), 1962; also Hans G. Furth, *Piaget and Knowledge,* Section III.
6. Felicie Affolter, "Developmental Aspects of Visual and Auditory Pattern Perception in Children," Unpublished Ph.D. Dissertation, The Pennsylvania State University, 1970.

movement is a primary example. He then develops schemes whereby he may take data from both of these senses to generate a correct response; grasping an object is an example.

According to Piaget's theory, schemes are developed to assimilate the stimulus into an overall structure of behavior, and the important thing about this function is not the stimulus nor the response but the cognitive processes developed to cope with this stimulus. These cognitive processes are hierarchically structured and integrated so that one can reason from one level to another and thus make intelligent decisions about stimuli he has not encountered before. A little thinking reveals that every communicative situation is different and thus requires slight modification of the behavior with which we respond. The degree to which we are able to modify our communicative behavior in varying situations may be an indication of the maturity of our cognitive structure. In thinking along these lines one should remember that schemes for dealing with stimuli can only be developed in the child in response to sensory input. Thus the diversity of experiences a child has in his developing years may well affect his ability to think constructively in later years.

Discuss the above hypothesis and its relation to I.Q.

The second prerequisite to language acquisition was that of symbolic functioning.[7] This is defined as the ability to role-play or imitate an action seen in others. It develops in stages from the ability to imitate a person's actions immediately after he has performed them, to the ability to remember this action and perform it sometime later, to the ability to "play" as though something resembling the real thing is really that thing (a stone becomes a piece of candy), to a full blown imagination that can transform any given object into something else. Thus a child learns to use symbols to evoke behaviors that could only be evoked by the real thing in a lower animal. This ability to develop along the above symbolic continuum seems to be innate and a prerequisite to language acquisition. Again varying abilities for symbolic functioning may predict varying abilities in linguistic performance.

Not only does one's ability in symbolic functioning predict one's verbal capabilities, but it also appears to be indicative of one's nonverbal sensitivity. Why should this be, and what are some of the ramifications of such a theory. The developmental stages a child goes through are based entirely upon the experience he has before he has any verbal ability. His senses of touch, taste, and smell play a great part in his very early experiences, as do his senses of sight and hearing. Through these experiences he develops his behavioral schemes which enable him to

7. Felicie Affolter, "Thinking and Language," in *International Research Seminar on the Vocational Rehabilitation of Deaf Persons,* Glenn Lloyd (ed.), Washington: Department of Health, Education and Welfare, 1968, pp. 116-123.

respond in acceptable ways to both verbal and nonverbal stimuli. Since he knows no words, he is responding primarily to the nonverbal cues he picks up from the behavior of those around him. The schemes he develops to assimilate these stimuli into his cognitive structure become the basic schemes for the entire hierarchy of cognitive processes. Thus their influence is the most basic influence we have. As we mature these basic influences get pushed further and further into the depths of our cognitive structures until we are no longer cognizant of their influence. Yet they continue to function on the subconscious level.

It takes a real effort to bring these basic perceptual schemes to the surface of our cognitive processes. Many times it is impossible. Yet, one need only reflect for a while on his own communicative behavior to realize that these influences are very active in his perception of others. The examples given in Chapter 3 should help you to recognize this. Further evidence comes from the present experimental investigations of nonverbal behavior during communication situations. It is reported that when two or more people are communicating, their bodies, and especially their facial expressions, become synchronized in their movements.[8] It seems apparent that our nonverbal cues are picked up at least equally well, but probably more readily than our verbal cues. True, we do not communicate much substantive information nonverbally, but in the majority of our everyday communication situations it is the affective information that is more important and most of this comes from the nonverbal code.

The child's ability to imitate the nonverbal behavior of others is his first sign of symbolic functioning. This nonverbal behavior becomes his symbol of the one he is imitating. As soon as this imitation can be delayed we realize that he has an image of this person constructed in his cognitive structure. This image is primarily nonverbal. All of the emotions are bound up in this nonverbal image. Our likes and dislikes, fears, and desires are triggered most often by nonverbal cues. This is undoubtedly because the schemes governing these mental states (as indicated in Chapter 4) are developed through the assimilation of nonverbal stimuli. It would appear, then, that a primary area of research for the human-communication theorist is in nonverbal communicative behavior. Much too little is being done in this area.

Discuss your own feelings about the nonverbal behavior of others. Try to figure out how you developed these feelings.

The third prerequisite to language acquisition is that of pattern recognition. Language may be defined as an organized body of sounds and/or symbols. The word "organized" implies that there are recogniz-

---

8. Douglas W. Huenergardt and Steven J. Financo, "Micromomentary Facial Expressions as Perceivable Signs," a paper given at the 55th Annual Meeting of the Speech Association of America, 1969.

able patterns structured in such a way that differences in structure become meaningful. Structural linguistics is that field of linguistics which tries to discern the patterns of sounds and/or symbols that are meaningful for any given language group. One way of looking at language is that it is the bridge between an infinite number of possible sounds and/or symbols and an infinite number of possible meanings.[9] Language itself is made up of several strata, each subsuming the strata beneath it.[10]   The most basic strata, the phonemic level, is a subset of the infinite number of possible sounds selected by a particular culture as those sounds that will be meaningful for them. The question of which came first—the culture or the language, is a moot question, and one that has occupied much of the cultural-linguists' time.[11]   The easiest way out is to say that they developed simultaneously.

This finite subset of sounds called phonemes is organized into more complex patterns called morphemes which in turn are organized into more complex patterns called lexemes, which are organized into more complex patterns called sememes (See Figure 11). Sememes are put together in various combinations to form the sentences we utter to evoke meaning in the mind of a listener. Thus we are able to go from an infinite number of possible sounds to an infinite number of possible meanings by using a finite code. One of the meaningful characteristics of this code is that it has a definite pattern. The structural rules are

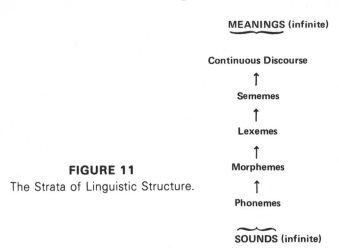

FIGURE 11
The Strata of Linguistic Structure.

MEANINGS (infinite)

Continuous Discourse
↑
Sememes
↑
Lexemes
↑
Morphemes
↑
Phonemes

SOUNDS (infinite)

9. Charles Hockett, *A Course in Modern Linguistics* (New York: The Macmillan Co., 1958).

10. Sydney M. Lamb, *Outline of Stratificational Grammar* (Washington: Georgetown University Press, 1966).

11. See Benjamin Lee Whorf, *Language, Thought, and Reality* (New York: John Wiley & Sons, Inc., 1962); and Harry Hoijer (ed.), *Language in Culture* (Chicago: The University of Chicago Press, 1954).

being studied by linguists. It is one of the most difficult tasks man has set for himself.

I am sure the reader is already confused by this simple statement about linguistic structure. Isn't it strange, then, that the child can learn all of these complicated organizations by the time he is five or six? One of the innate capacities a child must have is the ability to differentiate between patterns. He must be able to recognize patterns in order to learn speech. To learn a second language we have to learn another organization of similar speech sounds. The patterns exhibited in any language are the codes used to "carry" meaning. Chomsky has theorized that these surface codes have a deep structure that is less complex and more common to all languages.[12] Regardless of what theory of linguistics one chooses to follow he will find that their primary purpose is to find out the structure of the code we use to communicate on a verbal level. The point being made here is that as a child we learned this structure of sounds (perhaps two or more languages at once). Since we appear to attach more importance to this code for communication than to the nonverbal code, the human-communication theorist should know something about the linguistic theories which are attempting to describe the structure of this code.

Discuss various structures existing in written verbal material and their effect on meaning.

We have been talking about the three prerequisites to language learning and have seen how complex a code language is. Perhaps now would be a good time to take a brief look at what are considered to be the essential characteristics of a language. Hockett has set forth thirteen design-features that all languages share.[13]

Since all languages began as vocal utterances, they must have a (1) "vocal-auditory channel," that is, there must be some way to produce it and some way to receive this transmission. The second and third design-features are also characteristic of vocal transmission. They are, (2) "broadcast transmission and directional reception," that is, sound travels in all directions from the source but our ears and brain have the ability to detect the direction of the source of the transmission, and (3) "rapid fading," sound does not last. We must be within earshot at the moment the sound passes by or we will not receive the signal.

The fourth design-feature, "interchangeability," calls attention to the fact that "in general a speaker of a language can reproduce any linguistic message he can understand," so that there is an interchangeability between transmission and reception in terms of the code used. At the same time a speaker has (5) "total feedback" of everything relevant

12. Noam Chomsky, *Aspects of the Theory of Syntax* (Cambridge: The M.I.T. Press, 1965).

13. Charles Hockett, "The Origin of Speech," *Scientific American* (September, 1960), p. 88.

in the linguistic signal he transmits, for example, he hears his own signal and this is a very important part of the communication process. It is also important to note that the production of speech sounds is purely for the purpose of communicating. Hockett calls this (6) "specialization"; it is the special function of the speech mechanism, taken in its entirety, to produce communicative signals.

When we speak we use verbal units to specify particular elements of our perceived world. This (7) "semanticity" is the design-feature of language that makes it usable by more than one person. Though the referent of a verbal unit may have no direct relationship to that unit, one is still able to evoke relatively the same meaning in the minds of two or more listeners with the same word. The tie between a verbal unit and the semantic space it evokes is arbitrary. This (8) "arbitrariness" is the design-feature that gives language an unbounded power to reflect whatever elements become important to a culture. The name "dog" is arbitrary; so is rocket. Furthermore, the phonemic structure of the language is such that each specific phoneme in combination with other phonemes produces a specific verbal unit referring to its own specific referent. This (9) "discreteness" is what allows us to distinguish between "pin" and "pen."

Language allows us to talk about things from which we are separated in either time or space, or both. This (10) "displacement" feature allows us to take advantage of history and project into the future. It should also be apparent that we can produce strings of verbal units that we have never spoken before. This (11) "productivity" may be the most important feature of language because it means that we are not tied to a stimulus-response model, in that we can respond to any given situation in a wholly arbitrary way. We can produce a signal that is completely new to us and probably to the receiver. On the other hand, the ability to use language "correctly" can be taught because it is a common code among a number of people. Hockett calls this (12) "traditional transmission" because the conventions of language are transmitted from generation to generation through a teaching-learning situation. A child does not acquire just any language; he acquires the one common to the society he grows up in, whether it is the language of his parents or not.

The final design-feature, (13) that of "duality of patterning," is the feature that allows language to use a finite number of phonemes to produce a much larger body of meaningful sounds. The words "tack," "cat," and "act" all consist of the same three phonemes, but because they are arranged differently they evoke different meanings. It is seldom that a word is ambiguous because of its phonemic structure.[14]

---

14. Martha Kolln, "An Analytic and Experimental Study of the Information-Bearing Role of Stress-Unstress Patterns in English," Unpublished Master's thesis, The Pennsylvania State University, 1970.

The possibility that this might happen is virtually eliminated by the redundancy built into continuous discourse. Every word uttered has an expectancy factor associated with it. This expectancy factor is operative in both the encoding and the decoding of signals. It is best illustrated by playing the parlor game in which each successive person must add a meaningful word to the string already produced, with the restriction that it must make a grammatically acceptable utterance.

Discuss the importance of each of the design-features of language to the communication process.

It may be of interest to note that within the context of the above design-features one may distinguish between man and his nearest animal relative by indicating what the animals lack in the design-features of language. The Gibbons' call has all of the design-features except "displacement," they do not communicate about things that are not immediate; "productivity," they cannot "talk" about things that exist other than signal the existence of danger of physical necessities; "duality of patterning," their vocal patterns are not made up of permutations of a few phonemes; and possibly "traditional transmission," though it is conceivable that the young learn their calls from the old. The study of animal communication becomes relevant to the study of human communication only in the areas of overlap. It is questionable, then, whether we are learning more about animal communication because we know more about human communication, or vice versa. In either case, the human-communication theorist can profit by knowing what is known about animal communication.[15]

Language is, of course, one of the reasons why man claims to be an intelligent being. However, since it is an arbitrary symbol system, it has a built-in ambiguity factor. It is impossible to have one symbol for every shade of meaning, so we find the same symbol taking on many meanings. Homonyms only compound the difficulty. Besides this we find that many legitimate phrases have double meanings, such as, "How about a ride home?" Is he asking for a ride or offering a ride? Since linguistic symbols are used to direct the receiver's thought processes toward the desired meaning, it is only reasonable to assume that the receiver may misinterpret a direction here and there and thus arrive at the wrong meaning.

The importance of understanding the nature of language and the fact that meaning rests in the minds of the communicants and cannot be transferred from person to person should not be underestimated. However, neither should the commonality of our language system within our society be underestimated. This commonality makes it possible for us to communicate very well when we want to put the time and

15. See Stuart A. Altman, ed., *Social Communication Among Primates* (Chicago: University of Chicago Press, 1967) for an introduction to this subject.

effort required into it. This is evidenced by all of the movements which have developed over the extent of recorded history. People are motivated to beliefs and action by language, but we should not have the impression that all we need do is communicate and all our problems will cease. It is one thing to understand a person's message; it is quite another to agree with it. Only the former comes under the study of the human-communication process.

The field of General Semantics originated to study why man behaves the way he does in the communication situation. Alfred Korzybski is generally credited with having started this movement. It gained many adherents during the 1930's, '40's and '50's, and did much to move the speech discipline toward the study of the total communication situation. The basic premise upon which this school of thought is built seems to be that of awareness.[16] If we are aware of what is going on during the communication process, then we will be better able to evaluate the information obtained during this process. "Korzybski summarized, in a few simple and highly original formulations, what he felt to be the basic assumptions underlying the habits of evaluation common to the most advanced contemporary thinkers. The modern habits of evaluation appeared to rest, he said, on three fundamental 'non-aristotelian' premises. Comparing the relation of language (as well as of thought, memory, mental images) to reality with the relation of maps to the territory they represent, he laid down these premises: (1) a map *is not* the territory (words *are not* the things they represent); (2) a map *does not* represent *all* of a territory (words *cannot* say *all* about anything); (3) a map is *self-reflexive,* in the sense that an ideal map would have to include a map of the map, which in turn would have to include a map of the map of the map, etc. (it is possible to speak words about words, words about words about words, etc.; in terms of behavior this means it is possible to react to our reactions, react to our reactions to our reactions, etc.). Evaluative habits based on these premises, Korzybski said, result in flexibility of mind, lack of dogmatism, emotional balance and maturity, such as characterizes the best scientific minds—at least in their thought within their special fields."[17]

Relative to the premises stated above it is easy to see that our communicative behavior is not usually based upon them. We react to words as though they were the thing they represent. We are quick to stereotype a person or action on the basis of a few abstracted points rather than looking at the whole situation. We generally get caught up in our talking to the point that we talk because we are talking and often talk ourselves into positions and situations that we shouldn't be in. In short,

---

16. See J. Samuel Bois, *The Art of Awareness* (Dubuque: Wm. C. Brown Company Publishers, 1966), for a textbook on General Semantics.

17. S. I. Hayakawa, "Semantics," *ETC; A Review of General Semantics* (Vol. IX, No. 4, Summer, 1952), pp. 249–250.

we are seldom aware of our communicative behavior to the extent that we evaluate what we are doing as part of our evaluation of the whole communication process. Thus, our communicative behavior becomes rigid and we lose the ability to create new and more meaningful communication situations. On the other hand, many of us are so aware of our communicative behavior that we stifle this behavior to the point of reticence.[18] The optimal behavior, somewhere between introverted and extroverted behavior, is difficult to achieve but worthy of our efforts.

Discuss the effect a complete awareness would have on the communication process.

As we have tried to indicate in previous pages of this book, our communicative behavior must be defined as our verbal behavior plus our nonverbal behavior. Thus the entire self, as it is expressed in the way we walk, talk, dress, sit, stand, fix our hair, etc. etc. becomes our communicative behavior: the way we express ourselves in our everyday lives, the way others see us is the sum total of our communicative behavior.[19] Communication is the essence of man. He cannot live without it. Any time he is subjected to the behavior of others, he may conceive of this behavior as communicative behavior. Thus, when the television medium projects this behavior into his living room, it drastically affects his life and that of the society. Our behavior is communicative because it effects a change in the cognitive structure of another. Whatever we do that is perceived by another has communicated something to him. Since we do not know how our behavior will affect someone who does not know us, we can be sure that one-way communication will develop all kinds of misconception in the mind of the receiver. For example, T V accounts of the war in Southeast Asia and the 1968 Democratic convention were filled with confounding signals.

At the same time our behavior depends on our image of ourselves as well as that of the situation we are in.[20] How do we perceive ourselves in relation to the elements around us—whether they be people or inanimate objects? What does our attitudinal frame of reference have to do with the way we communicate? Much indeed. It has a major effect on the encoding process. Thus we communicate what we are in light of how we see the situation we are in. This means that our perceptual world also has a bearing on how we communicate.[21] Thus we analyze our audience, whether one person or many, to see how and in

18. Gerald Phillips, "The Problem of Reticence," *The Pennsylvania Speech Annual* (September, 1965), pp. 22-38.

19. Erving Goffman, *The Presentation of Self in Everyday Life* (Garden City: Doubleday-Anchor), 1959.

20. Kenneth E. Boulding, *The Image* (Ann Arbor: The University of Michigan Press, 1961).

21. Richard Gregg, "A Perceptual Approach to Rhetorical Study," a paper given at the Research Designs for General Semantics meeting, The Pennsylvania State University, March, 1969.

what signals our message should be coded. This analysis of the world out there is continuous and leads us to have a continual projected behavior. It is only when our expectancies are not met that we have to stop and think how we are going to behave. Our cybernetic continually brings the outside world into its computations to insure that we behave, communicatively, in the way we are expected to. We then become known by our behavior, and this is the ingredient we add to any communicative situation, whether we are conscious of it or not.

Discuss various cases where your perception of yourself or the outside world has limited your communicative behavior.

It should be clear that our perception of the situation will greatly affect the way we communicate in that situation. How is this influence manifested in our communicative behavior? Transactional analysis is a school of psychology specifically designed to study the interaction of human beings in communicative situations. The data gathered and analyzed by researchers holding to this school of thought indicate that much of human behavior may be looked at as game playing behavior. "A *Game* is an ongoing series of complementary ulterior transactions progressing to a well-defined, predictable outcome. Descriptively it is a recurring set of transactions, often repetitious, superficially plausible, with a concealed motivation; or, more colloquially, a series of moves with a snare, or 'gimmick.' "[22]   Prime examples are the "con game" and seduction. Thus our communicative behavior depends on our motives as well as our perceptions. A message is then encoded and the signal transmitted which will have the best chance of reaching our goals for that particular situation.

As we have indicated these signals may be verbal or nonverbal, and our nonverbal signals may say more about the real me than the verbal signals do. This is only too apparent in our use of two elements we all must deal with: time and space. These two universal variables in the communication process, if understood sufficiently, will tell us much about the people we communicate with. We are continually telling people about ourselves by being prompt or late for appointments, by doing a job quickly or "taking all day," by rising early or staying up late, etc. In the same way we project ourselves by the way we use space. Do we stand close to people when we talk, perhaps even touching them? Do we refuse to sit next to some people, or work in the same building with them? How about the way we decorate our rooms, and whether we live in an open area or crowded city? All of these things "say" something about us and are read by those who come in contact with us.[23] This area of research into human-communicative behavior is just

22. Eric Berne, *Games People Play* (New York: Grove Press, Inc., 1964), p. 48. Copyright © 1964 by Eric Berne.

23. See Edward T. Hall, *The Silent Language* (Greenwich, Conn.: Fawcett Publications, Inc., 1959), A Premier Book d117, 1959, and *The Hidden Dimension* (Garden City, New York: Doubleday & Company, Inc., 1966).

becoming popular, but it is certainly one of the most needed types of research in the field of human communication. We know very little about the nonverbal dimensions of communicative behavior.

Discuss what nonverbal cues you use to assess the character of those you meet.

Conclusion:

In the last few pages we have indicated some of the variables active in the human-communication process. We have said a little about the feelings of a person during the communication process and how these affect his communicative behavior. In a group setting one has to consider an individual's feelings about each of the other members of the group. What's more, this feeling bit should be carried at least one step farther and consider how you think the other person feels about you. Of course, one could go still further and consider how you think they think you feel about them and so on *ad infinitum,* the main point being that in any human interaction one must consider the multiple feelings of all those involved.

Since the days of Freud, man has been looking at the unconscious manifestations of the real self. One often asks himself, "What did he mean by that remark?" or "Why did he do that?" Until a few years ago the customary way to study human involvement was to probe the individual's mental makeup. Or, in a group situation, to look for the goals, the pressures, and the leadership characteristics of the group. More recently the trend has been to group psychotherapy, and one of the ways developed to approach these studies is called transactional analysis. The everyday use of this theory has been to see what roles people play in the relations they have with other people. Interpersonal relationships depend upon one's feelings about another as hereinbefore stated.

Shakespeare's proclamation that the whole world is a stage and every man is a player takes on more meaning as we come to understand the interpersonal relations of human beings. There are only short steps from drama to role playing to gamesmanship. We have seen that both verbal and nonverbal behavior may be communicative in human interaction. As to which is the more important, one must first answer the question, "Are you talking about the affective or the substantive level of communication?" Only on the substantive level is verbal behavior more productive than nonverbal behavior.

We have looked at the theory of games on an individual level; perhaps we should also consider this theory on a cultural or national level. Power moves and propaganda techniques are certainly calculated to elicit some type of reaction from other countries or people. In this sense we can include both of them under human communication. Since countries develop systems of control much like humans do, and their cybernetic is built up over a period of years, it is composed of many, if not all, of the same characteristics of the human system. This being the case, the study of cultural characteristics and systems should prove beneficial to the student of human communication.

Besides the general similarity of a culture to a human, there is also the role culture plays in the communicative behavior of an individual. Cultural norms, desires, and idiosyncrasies play a very definite role in the way a person perceives, interprets, and responds to a message. Think of the ways in which Americans differ from other people in their feelings about space. Our feelings about time, space, color, sound, and taste also differ from those of people of other cultures.

These differences manifest themselves in our art forms, our music, dance, literature, films, theater, and architecture. Each one of these manifestations is a coded message to the foreigner as well as to the native. They play a very important part in the communication situation.

The student of human communication should be aware of these differences and strive to understand how they affect communicative behavior. Then he should be able to see that subcultures within our own country may also exhibit differing characteristics. Thus, he should be able to foresee some of the difficulties that might arise in a communication situation. His ability to perceive these differences and interpret them correctly will facilitate his communication. His ability to use these nonverbal codes to create the desired message in the mind of his communicatee will enhance the effect of his communication.

Discuss the role of the above nonverbal codes in the way you perceive others.

BIBLIOGRAPHY

1. ALTMAN, STUART A., ed. *Social Communication Among Primates.* Chicago: University of Chicago Press, 1967.
2. ARDREY, ROBERT. *The Territorial Imperative.* New York: Atheneum Publishers, 1966.
3. BARKER, ROGER. *The Stream of Behavior.* New York: Appleton-Century-Crofts, 1963.
4. BELL, EARL H. *Social Foundations of Human Behavior.* New York: Harper & Row Publishers, 1961.
5. BERNE, ERIC. *Games People Play.* New York: Grove Press, Inc., 1964.
6. BOIS, J. SAMUEL. *The Art of Awareness.* Dubuque: Wm. C. Brown Company Publishers, 1966.
7. BOULDING, KENNETH E. *The Image.* Ann Arbor: The University of Michigan Press, 1961.

8. BROWN, ROGER. *Words and Things.* New York: Free Press of Glencoe, 1958.

9. CARROLL, JOHN B. *Language and Thought.* Englewood Cliffs, N.J.: Prentice-Hall, Inc., 1964.

10. CARTWRIGHT, DORWIN, and ZANDER, ALVIN. *Group Dynamics.* Evanston, Ill.: Row, Peterson and Co., 1960.

11. CHASE, STUART. *The Tyranny of Words.* New York: Harcourt, Brace & World, Inc., 1938.

12. CHOMSKY, NOAM. *Aspects of the Theory of Syntax.* Cambridge: The M.I.T. Press, 1965.

13. Ciba Foundation. *Disorders of Language.* Boston: Little, Brown and Co., 1964.

14. COMBS, ARTHUR, and SNIGG, DONALD. *Individual Behavior,* Rev. Ed. New York: Harper & Brothers, 1959.

15. DAVITZ, J. R., ed. *The Communication of Emotional Meaning.* New York: McGraw-Hill Book Co., 1964.

16. DEUTSCH, J. A. *The Structural Basis of Behavior.* Chicago: The University of Chicago Press, 1960.

17. DEUTSCH, KARL WOLFGANG. *The Nerves of Government.* London: Free Press of Glencoe, 1963.

18. DIXON, THEODORE R. and HORTON, DAVID L., eds. *Verbal Behavior and General Behavior Theory.* Englewood Cliffs: Prentice-Hall, Inc., 1968.

19. DUNCAN, HUGH D. *Communication and Social Order.* New York: Bedminster Press, 1962.

20. ————. *Symbols in Society.* New York: Oxford University Press, 1968.

21. FODOR, JERRY A., and KATZ, JERROLD J., eds. *The Structure of Language.* Englewood Cliffs: Prentice-Hall, Inc., 1964.

22. GOFFMAN, ERVING. *Encounters.* Indianapolis: The Bobbs-Merrill Co., Inc., 1961.

23. ————. *The Presentation of Self in Everyday Life.* Garden City: Doubleday-Anchor, 1959.

24. HALL, EDWARD T. *The Hidden Dimension.* Garden City: Doubleday & Company, Inc., 1966.

25. ————. *The Silent Language.* Greenwich, Conn.: Fawcett Publications, Inc., A Premier Book, d117, 1959.

26. HARE, PAUL; BORGOTTA, EDGAR; and BALES, ROBERT. *Small Groups.* New York: Alfred A. Knopf, Inc., 1962.

27. HARVEY, O. J. *Motivation and Social Interaction.* New York: The Ronald Press Co., 1963.

28. HAYAKAWA, S. I. *Language in Thought and Action.* New York: Harcourt, Brace and World, Inc., 1964.

29. HERTZLER, JOYCE. *A Sociology of Language.* New York: Random House, Inc., 1965.

30. HOCKETT, CHARLES. *A Course in Modern Linguistics.* New York: The Macmillan Co., 1958.

31. HOIJER, HARRY, ed. *Language in Culture.* Chicago: University of Chicago Press, 1954.

32. KATZ, ELIHU, and LAZARSFELD, PAUL. *Personal Influence.* Glencoe: Free Press, 1955.

33. KATZ, J. J., and POSTAL, P. M. *An Integrated Theory of Linguistic Descriptions.* Cambridge: The M.I.T. Press, 1964.

34. KNAPP, PETER H., ed. *Expression of the Emotions in Man.* New York: International Universities Press, 1963.

35. KORZYBSKI, ALFRED. *Science and Sanity.* Lakeville: International Non-Aristotelian Library, 1948.

36. LAMB, SYDNEY M. *Outline of Stratificational Grammar.* Washington: Georgetown University Press. 1966.

37. LEWIS, M. M. *Language, Thought and Personality in Infancy and Childhood.* New York: Basic Books, Inc., Publishers, 1963.

38. LURIA, ALEXANDER. *The Role of Speech in the Regulation of Normal and Abnormal Behavior.* New York: Liveright Publishing Corp., 1961.

39. MCNEIL, ELTON B. *The Nature of Human Conflict.* Englewood Cliffs: Prentice-Hall, Inc., 1965.

40. MEAD, GEORGE H. *Mind, Self and Society.* Chicago: University of Chicago Press, 1934.

41. NEUMEYER, ALFRED. *The Search for Meaning in Modern Art.* Englewood Cliffs: Prentice-Hall, Inc., 1964.

42. RIESMAN, DAVID; GLAZER, NATHAN; and DENNEY, REUEL. *The Lonely Crowd.* New Haven: Yale University Press, abridged edition, 1961.

43. RUESCH, JURGEN. *Therapeutic Communication.* New York: W. W. Norton Co., Inc., 1961.

44. —— and KEES, WELDON. *Non-Verbal Communication.* Berkeley: University of California Press, 1960.

45. RYCENGA, JOHN, and SCHWARTZ, JOSEPH. *Perspectives on Language.* New York: The Ronald Press Co., 1963.

46. SAPIR, EDWARD. *Culture, Language and Personality.* Berkeley: University of California Press, 1961.

47. ——. *Language.* New York: Harcourt, Brace & Co., 1921.

48. SAPORTA, SOL. *Psycholinguistics.* New York: Holt, Rinehart & Winston, Inc., 1961.

49. SCHRAMM, WILBUR. *Mass Communication*. Urbana: University of Illinois Press, 1960.
50. SEBEOK, THOMAS; HAYES, ALFRED; and BATESON, MARY, eds. *Approaches to Semiotics*. London: Mouton Co., 1964.
51. SKINNER, B. F. *Verbal Behavior*. New York: Appleton-Century-Crofts, 1957.
52. STAATS, ARTHUR, and STAATS, CAROLYN. *Complex Human Behavior*. New York: Holt, Rinehart & Winston, Inc., 1963.
53. ZIPF, G. K. *Human Behavior and the Principle of Least Effort*. Cambridge: Addison-Wesley Publishing Co., Inc., 1949.

Chapter 6

COMMUNICATIVE LITERACY: A POINT OF FOCUS

You all know what communication is; you've been doing it all your lives. But can you explain how and why you expend so much of your energy carrying on this activity? Can you think of a situation in which you would not be communicating to someone? To be is to communicate. Any entity, living or dead, will communicate at least this fact to those who come in contact with it. Herein lies the mystery of human communication. We can no more stop it from happening than we can stop breathing. We are constantly sending and receiving signals—modifying our own and others' view of reality. This process begins about nine months before birth and may continue for centuries after our death. It is a good intellectual exercise to determine what human behavior is *not* communicative behavior.

Such an all-pervasive activity must be of considerable importance to our development as a human being. I am sure you are at least semiconscious of the effect this activity has on your own understanding of the world around you. Undoubtedly you are also aware of the information explosion and its consequent effect on the activities of all mankind. Marshall McLuhan's name is most often associated with this knowledge. However, a brief look at history (as we have done in this book) reveals that man has always been inundated by an information explosion. Indeed it seems to be his nature to try and bury himself in such a mess. Our greatest desire seems to be to let other people know what we know. This book is a fitting example.

Man has always been in search of better ways to transmit information. We are constantly sending out signals for others to receive and reply to. Even when we do not want to do this, we are unable to stop. We are ever trying to find faster and more effective ways to transmit the information we feel others should have. At the same time we are constantly aware that the effectiveness with which we communicate is not only dependent upon the amount of information in the signal but also the way in which it is received and the code which conveys it. To say that we have communicated effectively is to say that the receiver of our signals *understands what we were trying to communicate.* Thus one aspect of human communication is understanding. To effect understanding we transmit a coded message as a signal in some medium. This may be spoken discourse which uses language as the code and air as the medium, or it may be emotional expression which uses art as the code and the canvas as its medium.

In any communication process the degree to which it is effective is dependent upon the degree of *competence* in the signal code *shared* by the sender and the receiver. Competence in signal codes is another way of saying literacy. Although literacy is usually equated with the ability to read and write, if we think of the implications of this ability, we are led to the broader meaning of the term—to be educated or acculturated. It takes only a simple extrapolation of this broader definition to equate it with one's ability to *create* or *decipher* a given communication code. We have now arrived at some simple constructs by which we may be able to apprehend the theories and concepts intrinsic to a study of man's communication process.

Communication is possible because man has developed a system of codes by which he can transmit information. A code is something that stands for something else, for example, in the Morse Code . . . stands for *S* and --- stands for *O*. In much the same way man uses language consisting of words and their positions relative to each other to stand for something else. Mary bit the dog, and the dog bit Mary, have the exact same words but stand for two entirely different happenings because of the position of the words relative to each other. The images that come to mind when we read the above two sentences are completely different but result from the same phenomenon and could have been evoked via a picture of the action. However, in neither of these examples does the reader have the real thing. Both of these examples illustrate the use of codes to evoke in the mind of the reader the message that was in the mind of the sender. The one code is language, the other is art.

Try to determine how many different codes man uses to communicate.

If you now have the idea of a code safely tucked away in your mind, let's take the next step and decide what determines which code should be used in any given communication situation. We must begin with the belief that in any communication situation we are trying to generate understanding in the mind of the receiver. This means that the receiver must receive a relatively pure signal (the composite of all the codes he is receiving). If there are extraneous signals being received, these will only confuse him in his attempt to arrive at the understanding intended by the sender. The following examples may clarify this point.

> I am listening to a mini-skirted graduate student expound on the meaning of meaning but cannot adequately differentiate between the signals I am receiving with my ears and those I am receiving with my eyes (as she squirms in her chair) to successfully evoke the message she is trying to communicate; or, I am reading a passage from "Paradise Lost" but cannot successfully differentiate between the signals I am receiving with my eyes from those I am receiving from my ulcer, thus, diminishing the richness of the message Milton wanted me to get; or, I am listening to my child tell me why he received such poor grades on his report card, but I cannot adequately differentiate between the signals picked up by my ears and those being generated by my mind thinking about all the things I should be doing instead of listening to him make excuses.

The above examples illustrate the use of language as a code and the way in which it may be confounded by other stimuli bombarding our senses. *Think of other codes and see if you can generate examples of how they might be confounded.*

In the process of doing the above exercise you may find that some codes are more relevant to specific communication situations than are others. It should be immediately clear to you that one of the reasons for the choice of one code over another is the ability of the sender and the receiver to understand this code, or it may rest only on the competency of the sender. It should also be clear that there are two halves to literacy. One is the ability to create and encode a message into a transmittable signal plus competency in transmission of the signal. The other is the reception and decoding of the signal and understanding the resulting message. It should be immediately clear that some of us are extremely literate in the use of some codes while extremely illiterate in the use of others. We may also find that we are all able to do various parts of this process with some codes better than we are able to do it with others, that is, you may be able to understand French but not speak it. A brief look at the development of literate man may help us to understand why.

Man's performance down through the ages has been governed by his literacy level. In his book, *Preface to Plato*, Eric Havelock makes the point quite clear that because earliest man was only literate in the spoken word, all business had to be transacted by word of mouth, and in order to guarantee the accuracy of these transactions over a period of time, they were committed to memory using the highly restrictive, but accurate, poetic form. He says,

> It was of the essence of Homeric poetry that it represented in its epoch the sole vehicle of important and significant communication. It therefore was called upon to memorialize and preserve the social apparatus, the governing mechanism, and the education for leadership and social manage-

ment, to use Plato's words. It is not only that Agamemnon, for example if he had to muster a fleet at Aulis might be compelled to get his directives organized in rhythmic verse so that they could remain unaltered in transmission. This same verse was essential to the educational system on which the entire society depended for its continuity and coherence. All public business depended on it, all transactions which were guided by general norms. The poet was in the first instance society's scribe and scholar and jurist and only in a secondary sense its artist and showman. . . .

Thus even the language of Euripides is still woven to a surprising degree out of the conventions of oral utterance. With the advance of literacy, the ceremonial style lost its functional purpose and hence its popular appeal, but to the end of the fifth century the role of the poet as society's encyclopedist, and the function of his formulaic speech as the vehicle of the cultural tradition, remain discernible and important.[1]

The above conjecture seems to have abundant support. Our most human aspect is speech with its necessary verbal patterns and its ability to evoke understanding in the mind of the receiver. However, it is a tribute to man's genius that he developed an alphabet and cultivated the ability to translate spoken discourse into written copy. All succeeding accomplishments of man have been predicated on this important breakthrough.

The invention of the alphabet in the eighth century B.C. added a new dimension to educated man. Though the addition of the new dimension called writing came slowly, it brought with it a very tangible discrimination between educated and uneducated man. We see this exemplified every day in young children who have just learned to read. As publishing facilities increased, the need to be literate and the status of the literate individual played a greater role in the development of society. Today, though there are still some languages that have not been committed to writing, and some people who have not learned to read or write a language, the illiteracy level is continually dropping.

What does this mean in terms of human communication? As we see in the everyday development of our own children, the ability to read and write greatly facilitates their use of language and their understanding of their fellowman. The fact that history and literature abound in the written form means that one can accumulate a vast knowledge of man to aid him in his own encounters with man. The accumulation of knowledge in this way should greatly enhance one's ability to function as a social being. Unfortunately, many times it does not. Though many of us are highly literate in the visual-verbal mode (writing-reading), we are often illiterate or only semi-literate in the vocal-verbal mode (speaking-listening). Thus the addition of another dimension to man's knowledge-gathering abilities not only expanded his possibilities for

1. Eric Havelock, *Preface to Plato* (Cambridge: Harvard University Press, 1963), pp. 93-95.

becoming a social being, but it also gave his fellowman another measure of his intellectual accomplishments and thus subjected him to a more rigorous examination before social approval. More emphasis is now being placed on one's ability to read and write than his ability to speak and listen.

These same developmental characteristics are true of other modes of human interaction. We need only mention them for you to see the analogous development. Much can be learned about man through his use of such codes as mathematics, music, art, and dance. All of these codes are as old as man himself. His use of such codes to convey messages is commonly accepted and the concept of literacy is readily applied. Perhaps something could be said of the fact that of our five commonly accepted codes, such as, language, mathematics, music, dance, and art, only art has never had a preliterate existence. The fact that art exists means that it was recorded for others to decipher. The other four codes have all existed in pre-literate man. (Literate now being used to mean one's ability to read and write this code.) In fact it has only been in the past fifty years that acceptable ways for writing dance code have been invented.

A curious phenomenon about literacy in any of the five codes is that, though literacy is usually assumed to mean the ability to read and write, in our present society if we make any pretense of being literate at all, we emphasize the reading ability over the writing ability. This phenomenon takes on strange shapes as we trace it through the five codes. Originally it was assumed that all humans were artists of one degree or another just as they could all speak with some degree of proficiency. When the alphabet came into common use for the recording of important factual matters, then both art and poetry became less essential to the welfare of society and were developed as an art form of expression. A subset of humanity began to cultivate these modes of expression and only they became proficient in the coding process. The same is true of the other codes to some degree. Though nearly all humans learn to write verbal discourse, most are not proficient to the point of being considered a writer. We are all aware of this phenomenon in mathematics, music, and dance.

The ability to decipher or get the message from these codes, once they have been recorded and the signal received by the communicatee, is far more existent than the ability to create these codes. In the case of music and dance (language also if we consider theater), this is a two-step process. Most of the time the writer is not the performer. Even so, the literacy level of decoding is much more extant than that of encoding. It would appear that the more affluent society becomes, the higher the levels of literacy get to be on both ends of the communication process. However, the cultivation of one's ability to appreciate the humanistic output of the various disciplines arising around these five codes is increasing much more rapidly than the development of one's creative skills.

Discuss the inequities in the two parts of literacy.

Conclusion

We would like to emphasize again the difficulties involved in becoming literate in any given mode of discourse, regardless of which code we are using. Most of us have some degree of literacy with each code mentioned—either in creating, deciphering, or both. Whereas, we usually think that in the vocal-verbal mode of discourse one is as proficient a creator as he is a decipherer, this should not be taken for granted. In each instance, and for all codes, each individual falls at a different place on the literate-illiterate continuum. As we work our way up these continua for each code, and each side of the communication schema, we become a more functional human being. These developmental characteristics of human growth are the key to the study of the human-communication process.

BIBLIOGRAPHY

1. ALSTON, WILLIAM. *Philosophy of Language.* Englewood Cliffs, N.J.: Prentice-Hall, Inc., 1964.

2. BECKER, ERNEST. *The Birth and Death of Meaning.* New York: The Free Press of Glencoe, 1962.

3. CASSIRER, ERNST. *The Philosophy of Symbolic Forms,* (Three Volumes). New York: Yale University Press, 1953-1957.

4. CHRISTENSEN, NIELS, E. *On the Nature of Meaning.* Copenhagen: Munksgaard, 1961.

5. COHEN, L. JONATHAN. *The Diversity of Meaning.* London: Methuen & Co., Ltd., 1962.

6. GENDLIN, EUGENE. *Experiencing and the Creation of Meaning.* New York: The Free Press of Glencoe, 1962.

7. LANGER, SUSANNE K. *Philosophy in a New Key.* New York: The New American Library, 1948.

8. OGDEN, C. K. and RICHARDS, I. A., *The Meaning of Meaning.* New York: Harcourt, Brace & Co., 1952.

9. RUSSELL, BERTRAND. *An Inquiry into Meaning and Truth.* London: G. Allen and Unwin, Ltd., 1940.

INDEX